CURRENT

WHAT MAKES A HERO?

What Makes a **HERO?**

THE SURPRISING SCIENCE OF SELFLESSNESS

ELIZABETH SVOBODA

CURRENT

CURRENT
Published by the Penguin Group
Penguin Group (USA) Inc., 375 Hudson Street
New York, New York 10014, USA

USA | Canada | UK | Ireland | Australia | New Zealand | India | South Africa | China

Penguin Books Ltd, Registered Offices: 80 Strand, London WC2R 0RL, England
For more information about the Penguin Group visit penguin.com

Copyright © Elizabeth Svoboda, 2013

Library of Congress Cataloguing in Publication Data

Svoboda, Elizabeth.
  What makes a hero? : the surprising science of selflessness / Elizabeth Svoboda.
    pages cm
  Includes bibliographical references.
  ISBN 978-1-59184-528-7 (hardback)
  1. Altruism. 2. Courage. 3. Heroes—Psychology. I. Title.
  BF637.H4S86 2013
  155.2'32—dc23   2013017671

Printed in the United States of America
1 3 5 7 9 10 8 6 4 2

31088100801602

Book design by Daniel Lagin
Set in Warnock Pro

To my parents, my first heroes

Contents

CONTENTS

PART II
PRACTICE

WHAT MAKES A HERO?

Introduction
CAN ANYONE BECOME A HERO?

t was a sunny summer day just outside Houston, Texas, and Shirley Dygert was getting ready to skydive for the first time. Dygert didn't fit the typical daredevil mold; she was a grandmother and longtime employee of the U.S. Postal Service. But her son lived close to a popular drop zone, and a couple years before—on his thirtieth birthday—he'd taken the plunge from 13,500 feet. He'd been raving about the experience ever since. So when Dygert's other son invited her to come along on his first dive, she readily agreed. When Dygert's party was summoned, she started to get nervous. "I thought, *OK, don't think about what you're about to do.*"

But when she met her instructor, Dave Hartsock—the man she'd be strapped to as they executed a tandem dive—she felt at ease. He seemed really interested in getting to know her, interrupting his stream of friendly chitchat only to provide reassuring answers to her questions. When she asked him how often he'd done this before, he reassured her, "Hundreds of jumps." She'd already done the most dangerous thing she would do all day, he told her: driving her car to the drop zone. By the time Dygert finally stepped out of the small plane into thin air, her fears had calmed a little.

For a few seconds that stretched long enough to seem like minutes, the dive went exactly as scripted. During the first phase, a free fall, all Dygert could do was gape at the spectacle of the Texas plains rising up to meet her, poised, it seemed, to envelop her in a comforting embrace when she touched down.

But problems started as soon as Hartsock opened the parachute to stop the free fall. The chute was supposed to billow out on all sides, but it didn't open all the way; instead, it stayed crumpled, like a discarded napkin. Around the same time, Hartsock and Dygert began to spin in midair. "We went around in a circle and we just kept going," Dygert remembers. "Dave said, 'I'll be honest with you. We're in trouble.'"

Ordinarily, the failure of the primary parachute wouldn't have presented a serious problem. Most skydiving teams are equipped with a backup chute, which the instructor can deploy by pulling a handle. But when Hartsock fired the backup chute, it got all tangled up with the primary parachute. So he started manipulating the snarled parachute lines to try to slow their fall. "I just grabbed a bunch of lines," he says, "and started pulling."

After a few seconds, though, it became clear that Hartsock's emergency backup measures weren't working well enough. He and Dygert were still falling toward the ground—and falling fast. Certain that she was going to die, Dygert frantically tried to locate her family on the ground so she could tell whether or not they were watching. She didn't want them to have to see this.

When Dygert and Hartsock were still a few hundred feet from the ground, Hartsock made a fateful—and very conscious—decision: He used control toggles to rotate himself in the air so that he was underneath Dygert. That way, his body would cushion her fall and she'd have a chance to survive even if his own odds of making it were low. But he didn't explain his reasoning to her. Instead, he gave her a swift, direct instruction. "I told her to pull up her legs."

Hartsock's split-second midair decision dramatically altered the course of both his life and his student's. After the two of them hit the ground with a sickening *crunch*, Dygert slowly tried to reorient herself. She couldn't believe she was still alive. "I looked over my shoulder. Dave was on the ground, and I was lying on top of him." She hoped Hartsock had avoided the worst, but as more people began to run to the scene, it dawned on her that he was in for a rough time. "A kid from our party said, 'Get off him. He's not breathing.'"

Though Dygert kept telling everyone she felt fine, doctors determined she'd broken multiple vertebrae in her neck and sustained other internal injuries. But that was nothing, she later learned, compared with what had happened to Hartsock. When he regained consciousness, he faced a rude awakening: His spinal cord had been injured and he was paralyzed from the neck down. In all likelihood, he'd never walk again, much less jump 13,500 feet from a plane.

It took Dygert some time to realize the magnitude of the sacrifice her teacher had made. At first, she figured it was mere chance that Hartsock, and not she, had been the one to sustain permanent paralysis. "I sure would have split it with him," she remembers thinking wistfully. But it soon became clear that her own narrow escape had been no accident. A man who'd just met her had sacrificed his own health and well-being so she might be able to keep hers. "I was absolutely amazed," Dygert says, blinking back tears. "How can somebody have that much love for another person?"

The question that still preoccupies Dygert is the same one that echoed in so many people's minds after the story of Hartsock's feat went public. *Why?* Why did Dave Hartsock—going against every self-preserving impulse that must have screamed through him—propel his body in a direction he knew would put him in harm's way? It's one thing to talk about putting your life on the line for someone else, but it's quite another to actually *do* it, as Hartsock did. As Miep Gies did when she hid Anne Frank and her family during the Holocaust. As Wesley Autrey did when he jumped off a New York City subway platform in 2007 to save a man who'd stumbled onto the tracks. How *can* someone have that much love for another person—enough to put that person's well-being and survival ahead of their own?

Traditionally, we have turned to the realm of the sublime to address questions like these—to deep moral contemplation, to the practice of spiritual discipline. But researchers from all over the world are turning the exacting lens of science on altruism and heroism for the first time. Not only are they exploring how biology, upbringing, and outside influences intersect to produce selfless and heroic behavior, they're investigating ways we can encourage this behavior in corporations, in organizations, in classrooms, and in individuals. In short, they're focusing on what makes a Dave Hartsock and on making sure future generations include plenty of them, too. Can *you*—can any ordinary person—learn to build on your natural biological endowments to turn yourself into a model of selflessness and service to others? Plenty of scientists and experts are now staking their careers on that possibility.

But new attempts to suss out the origins of selflessness and encourage it raise additional questions. What makes a hero, anyway? The psychologist and Stanford professor emeritus Phil Zimbardo is obsessed with finding out. The architect of the famed Stanford Prison Experiment—in which college students assigned to be "guards" lorded it over unfortunate "prisoners"—Zimbardo proved that perfectly normal people can act downright sadistic under certain conditions. He spent years exploring the situational genesis of human evil. But a few years ago, while writing his book *The Lucifer Effect*, he began to weary of the dark side. "I was so depressed, being immersed in the Stanford prison study. I realized, I've done fifteen chapters of the worst in human nature. So the last chapter is 'How do we resist these negative influences, and how do we celebrate heroism?'"

That final chapter proved the catalyst for a career turnaround, inspiring Zimbardo to devote his in-depth knowledge of human behavior to studying the origins of heroism. To jump-start his new project, he wanted to understand what people really thought qualified as heroism, so he appealed to the wisdom of the crowd. He put out a call for survey participants on the popular blog Boing Boing and elsewhere, presenting more than 3,600 respondents with a variety of potentially heroic situations. He and his colleagues asked the respondents to rate the examples as heroic, altruistic, or neither. In other items, they rated people's behavior on a continuum from "not at all heroic" to "extremely heroic."

The situations that received the highest heroism scores in Zimbardo's survey involved some kind of high-stakes sacrifice or rescue similar to the one Hartsock carried out. About 9 in 10 responders stated that civilian fire rescuers and soldiers who gave their lives were heroic. (Civilian fire rescuers were actually rated slightly *more* heroic than soldiers—perhaps because they perform their work voluntarily rather than out of duty, as soldiers do. Soldiers also kill people in addition to saving them.) In fact, after word got out about what Hartsock had done, people responded just as the Boing Boing survey-takers did, instantly recognizing his self-sacrificing act as heroic. The journalist Steve Hartman profiled Hartsock on CBS News and kudos began to pour in from around the world.

Zimbardo and his Medical College of Wisconsin colleague Zeno Franco found that physical heroes like Hartsock receive somewhat higher heroic ratings than so-called social heroes, who may not sacrifice their physical safety but who still put their comfort or livelihood on the line for a community value greater than themselves. Erin Brockovich-Ellis, who exposed the Pacific Gas and Electric Company's introduction of toxic chemicals into Southern California groundwater, is a social hero. So is Ted Johnson, the former New England Patriots linebacker who went public with the devastating after-effects of his football head injuries in order to save others from his fate, even though he knew he'd face embarrassment and a backlash from detractors and league officials. "Social heroism has potential to create real change," Franco says. "That seems like it should be as important as someone who risks their life for someone else."

In addition, most of the survey participants saw a distinct difference between heroism and altruism—the difference between Dave Hartsock and Volunteer of the Year award winners. "Altruism, you are helping others out of morality and unselfishness. Heroism is the same except in more extreme situations such as saving a life," one respondent explained. "Altruism seems to involve helping a group of people directly—there is a sacrifice, but it is more sharing what you have than sacrificing yourself," another wrote.

The quest to define different kinds of selflessness reminded me of what happened to a boy in my high school class. At the end of our sophomore year, he was hanging out with some friends on a railroad bridge, and the group saw a train approaching in the distance. They quickly scrambled off—all except for the boy's girlfriend. Her foot had gotten stuck in the tracks, and she was struggling to get away. The boy returned to the tracks to help free her, but time ran out; the oncoming train struck them both. In the days that followed, many people praised the boy's uncommon courage, and later, the class dedicated a page in the yearbook to him. We had known this boy as a lighthearted jokester (he'd been voted "class jester" in middle school), as a mischief maker, as a friend and confidant—in short, as a complex and multilayered human being. Now, all of a sudden, he was gone, and almost immediately afterward, he was anointed a hero. All of this happened so quickly we had trouble processing it. Yet the last act of his life had undeniably been heroic, and it got me wondering just how you became a hero. I knew heroism traditionally involved a significant element of personal sacrifice. Was carrying out one transcendent, self-abnegating act the only way to achieve heroic status? Or could you assemble a heroic identity like a puzzle, piece by piece, over time?

I've thought about these questions quite a bit in the years since and still don't have any straightforward answers. The kind of awe-inspiring sacrifice my classmate showed—heroism in the classical sense—is a very real phenomenon, one to be admired and emulated. Similarly, social heroes who operate all over the world receive deserved recognition for their work. In general, heroism as classically defined involves a much higher degree of risk or sacrifice than altruism, and while altruists typically receive accolades from the community, physical and social heroes must often sacrifice their lives or their status in order to defend principles they believe in.

My hunch, though, is that many slow-and-steady career altruists also practice a kind of quiet heroism, one that too often goes unrecognized. These people may never execute death-defying rescues or make the front page of the newspaper, but they make real sacrifices in terms of time and personal investment, and their unselfish contributions have genuine power to change the world. Take Jeff Bornefeld, my own mentor and friend, who has devoted much of his life to running a Northern California mentoring program for at-risk youth. To keep the program going, he spends multiple days each month away from his wife back in Portland, Oregon. Few people outside the Bay Area know his name, but to the hundreds of youth who have participated in his program over the years, he is unquestionably a hero. As Zimbardo says, "There is a fine line at the upper limit of altruism that blends into heroism."

Not only does Zimbardo view ultradedicated altruists as heroic in their own right, he believes there is an essential connection between small selfless deeds and larger ones—that altruism in the daily, low-key sense ("heroism lite") may help prepare us for later heroic intervention by training us to focus on others' needs. He believes meaningful opportunities for selflessness can exist in the most ordinary places: on the walk from the subway to the office, in a corporate boardroom crammed with suit-clad executives, and in the bedroom of a slowly dying loved one who can no longer inhale a full deep breath. It makes sense to me, then, to view heroism and altruism not as completely distinct quantities but as related hues in a single broad spectrum of generosity. Few of us would disagree that an Oskar Schindler who puts his own life in danger to save thousands of people from near-certain death is on a different plane from a volunteer who spends some time each week helping build homes for displaced people, or a low-paid intern who donates part of her hard-earned paycheck to charity. But all of these acts arise from the same basic motivation—enriching someone else's life at personal expense, whether small or large—so the differences between them are, in part, a matter of degree.

Besides broadening traditionally narrow definitions of heroism, researchers are proposing that behaving heroically may be a more accessible goal than many people think. There's a widespread cultural assumption that heroes are *born* remarkable, like Athena emerging full-fledged from the head of Zeus. Our religious and folk narratives often perpetuate this assumption: Jesus, for instance, is said to have been divine even when he was laid in a Bethlehem manger, and fictional heroes like Hercules and Paul Bunyan are portrayed as having been born with remarkable physical capabilities.

My initial look at selflessness science, on the other hand, hinted that we have ample opportunity to *choose* altruism or heroism, much as Dave Hartsock and my high school classmate did. This is true not just in high-stakes, split-second situations, but over the entire course of our lives. To be a hero, "historically, you have to have some special skill that goes above and beyond what ordinary people have. That's a leftover from our distant past," Franco says. "We've moved from that position. What we're saying is that *anyone* can be a hero."

The political theorist Hannah Arendt's doctrine of the "banality of evil" states that ordinary people are capable of evil under the wrong circumstances. But the "banality of heroism"—a term Zimbardo popularized—implies the flip side: everyone is capable of sacrificing for the greater good in some significant way, regardless of life circumstances, physical strength, worldview, or past actions. But are Zimbardo and Franco right? Can anyone really become a hero?

PART I
THEORY

Chapter One
IN THE GENES?

Krom was thirsty, and it seemed like there was nothing she could do about it. A rubber tire filled with water dangled tantalizingly from a climbing log overhead, but though the elderly chimpanzee had pulled and pushed on the tire for more than ten minutes to try to get it off the log, her efforts were in vain. There were six other heavy tires hanging on the log in front of the water-filled one, thwarting her fiercest attempts to jerk it free. Resigned to her failure, she began to walk away.

Another chimpanzee, seven-year-old Jakie, stood nearby. He knew Krom well—they had lived together for years at the Arnhem Zoo, and Krom had helped care for Jakie when he was a young chimp. As the primatologist Frans de Waal tells it, his colleague Otto Adang watched as Jakie sauntered over to the log. He reached up and pushed each of the heavy tires off it, one at a time, until only the water-filled tire was left. Like a young initiate paying tribute to a respected elder stateswoman, he eased the tire off the log and carried it over to Krom, making sure it stayed upright so that none of the liquid spilled out. Joyfully, Krom dipped her hands into the water and began scooping it into her mouth.

———

Anuradha Koirala once came home every day to a partner who hit her until she was black and blue. The former Nepalese English teacher suffered three miscarriages, which she thinks may have occurred as a result of the beatings.

After she summoned up the strength to get out of her abusive relationship, Koirala resolved to dedicate her life to saving other women trapped in the prison of abuse. Every year, she knew, thousands of Nepalese girls were sold into sex slavery in India, some who hadn't even gone through puberty yet. Koirala's job paid a salary of about $100 a month, and she used part of that money to start a shop that employed women who'd managed to escape from the brothels where they were being held.

The shop did well, but as time went by, Koirala was determined to step up her efforts. The sex-trafficking problem continued without respite, leaving thousands of physically and psychologically scarred women in its wake. Many of these women were viewed as ruined in Nepal, particularly if they'd contracted AIDS or another sexually transmitted disease while in their captors' custody. Wanting to give them a chance to reemerge as productive, fulfilled members of society, Koirala started an organization called Maiti, which means "Mother's Home."

When a woman arrives at one of the Maiti rehabilitation centers, she receives medical treatment and counseling if she needs it, but she is also given space to recover on her own timetable. "When the girl first comes to Maiti Nepal, we never, never ask them a question. We just let them [be] for as long as they need. We let them play, dance, walk, talk to a friend," Koirala told the CNN reporter Ebonne Ruffins in 2010. Recovered victims of sex slavery sometimes work as counselors at the centers, helping prepare other women to reenter society. In addition to victims of sex trafficking, Koirala continued, her facilities take in abandoned children and victims of rape and domestic violence. "I cannot say no to anybody. Everybody comes to Maiti Nepal."

In animals as well as in humans, helping behavior like Jakie's and Koirala's is surprisingly common, ingrained into our biological makeup as surely as height, hair texture, and eye color. Bonobos come to the aid of other injured bonobos, ravens call to other members of their species to share the spoils of a carcass they've found, and meerkats stand guard to allow others in the pack to search for food. What's more, these generous instincts may be even stronger in humans than in their mammalian counterparts. Eighteen-month-old toddlers in a study at Germany's Max Planck Institute, too young to be cognizant of "appropriate" social behavior, moved almost reflexively to hand experimenters clothespins that were out of reach and assisted them in restacking piles of books (though some of this early selflessness may have arisen through modeling parental behavior).

But even if we accept that unselfishness may have biological origins, we're left with the staggering question of why. A cursory read of Darwinian evolutionary doctrine suggests that the selfish individuals able to outcompete others for the best mates and the most resources are most likely to pass their genes on to the next generation. In this survival-of-the-fittest light, a bonobo that stops to help a wounded bonobo and leaves himself vulnerable to predators doesn't seem magnanimous; he just seems a little dim. What's more, it's clear that living creatures aren't inclined to behave unselfishly all the time. Animals may fight to the death to acquire dominance within social colonies, and humans have waged wars in the name of territorial conquest for nearly all of recorded history. Yet generosity, too, has persisted, demanding an explanation for its existence. Why do any living creatures—let alone you and I—behave self-sacrificially at all?

WHAT MAKES A HERO?

This was a question that obsessed Charles Darwin from the time he devised his theory of evolution. He was convinced that the fittest individuals, the ones best adapted to their environment, should reign supreme in the race to propagate offspring. Honeybees, though, gave him pause. When Darwin pondered the structure of bee colonies, he noted that they contained large numbers of sterile worker bees who toiled tirelessly to serve the queen of the colony. These workers did not have a chance to pass on genes to their own offspring, but spent their lives gathering pollen or feeding the queen so that she could reproduce.

On the surface, this scenario seemed to defy the laws of natural selection, and bothered Darwin greatly. He was concerned that such altruism in the animal kingdom could invalidate his evolutionary theory. While he wasn't ready to scrap his ideas, he was perturbed enough to note that sterile worker insects presented a problem "which at first appeared to me insuperable, and actually fatal to the whole theory."

Darwin wrestled with the sterile-insect problem for quite some time before arriving at what he considered one evolutionary explanation for it. He concluded that the worker bees doted on the queen because they were close kin to her. The problem of altruistic sterile insects, he noted, vanishes when you consider that selection can work on a family as well as an individual level. So while the workers might be committing reproductive hara-kiri due to their asexual lifestyle, their actions ensured that their own kind would be perpetuated—even if another closely related individual, the queen, was doing the actual passing on.

While Darwin argued that altruism in the animal world could be explained at least in part by family ties, his contemporary Peter Kropotkin, a Russian biologist and anarchist, believed that animals had a survival incentive to help others of their kind even if those others weren't related to them. A fan of *On the Origin of Species* since reading it as a young man, Kropotkin devoted his life to studying how evolution worked, and as a sergeant in the Russian military, he opted for a post in Siberia, which fired his imagination because it was largely unexplored territory.

In *The Altruism Equation*, the evolutionary biologist Lee Dugatkin recounts how in this cold, sparsely populated climate, Kropotkin witnessed many instances of spontaneous helping behavior in the animal communities of the area. Large animals formed herds to stay warm and to help one another find sustenance. Burying beetles collaborated in dragging the corpses of dead mice or birds to soft ground, then they all pitched in to bury the corpse so some of the beetles could lay their eggs inside. (Burying shielded the corpse from competitors so that it would serve as a reliable food source for the newly hatched larvae.) "I saw mutual aid and mutual support carried on to an extent," Kropotkin wrote, "which made me suspect in it a feature of the greatest importance for the maintenance of life, the preservation of each species and its further evolution."

Kropotkin, however, saw no direct connection between an animal's altruism and its familial relatedness to the animal it was helping. He acknowledged that life was a continual struggle to survive. But he saw cooperation as an integral part of the natural world because of the harsh realities of nature, not in spite of them. He believed animals had a strong biological imperative to help others of their kind because such strategies improved the survival odds of every individual in the group. "There is an immense amount of warfare and extermination going on amidst various species; there is, at the same time, as much, or perhaps even more, of mutual support, mutual aid, and mutual defense," he wrote. "Sociability is as much a law of nature as mutual struggle."

Over the following century, these respective explanations for helping behavior would inspire two increasingly complex schools of scientific thought—one arguing that altruism existed because it helped ensure the survival of close kin, the other arguing that it existed because it improved the survival odds of members of a group. One strong proponent of the former theory was the British evolutionary biologist W. D. Hamilton, who formalized the concept of kin selection in mathematical terms.

Given to scribbling diagrams and formulae into his notes to help him understand abstract concepts, Hamilton distilled kin selection into an inequality called Hamilton's Rule. He structured this rule as $r \times b > c$, with r being the genetic relatedness between two animals, b being the reproductive benefits of behaving altruistically, and c being the reproductive cost of doing so. In other words, if a gene that promotes altruism is to thrive, the cost of acting altruistically needs to be lower than the benefits the altruist receives in return, which are partially determined by the altruist's genetic relationship to the beneficiary. As long as the altruist's genetic material persists over time in subsequent generations, one animal's sacrifice on behalf of its family group will prove "worth it" in evolutionary terms.

To understand how this kin selection principle works, imagine a bird sounding a warning cry to alert its relatives to a predator's presence. In the process of sending the alarm, the bird runs a high risk of revealing its position to predators and getting eaten. But if that alarm cry saves a dozen of the bird's close genetic relatives from a similar fate, more of the alarm-raising bird's genetic material will survive to make it to the next generation, even if the bird itself dies. Therefore, despite sacrificing its own interests for those of its relatives, the bird will have been a rousing genetic success—just like the bees who sacrifice their own reproductive prospects to ensure the success of the closely related queen.

As Dugatkin notes, kin selection theory still holds a lot of sway in the scientific world. In 1981, the University of Cape Town zoologist

Jenny Jarvis wrote a paper for *Science* describing the existence of large numbers of nonreproductive females in mole rat colonies; she speculated that the rats in the colony might all be members of an extended family lineage. About a decade later, the Cornell biologist Hudson Reeve and his colleagues confirmed that members of mole rat colonies were, in fact, highly genetically related to one another—a finding that appeared to validate the view that sacrifice on behalf of relatives can be a shrewd evolutionary strategy. The female mole rats themselves may not have been reproducing, but they helped support the well-being of close relatives that were, ensuring that genes very similar to their own would be passed on.

Over the years, though, various researchers have also highlighted the merits of the view that helping may maximize the survival odds of each member of a society. According to the theory now known as group selection, groups where many members possess traits that are not necessarily favorable on an individual level—such as a tendency toward cooperation or selflessness—may still be able to outreproduce other groups over time. That would mean that behaving less selfishly isn't just a way of protecting close family members; it might also be a way for individuals to improve their own prospects by contributing to the well-being of a strong collective.

How might group selection play out? Take the case of William Muir, an animal breeder at Purdue University who was trying to produce better chickens. One way to approach the problem would be to pick out the chickens that were individually the best egg-layers, and then breed them in order to concentrate high-egg-production genes in the population. But Muir found that when the chickens with great egg-production pedigrees were taken out of their group cages and bred together, the aggressive offspring clawed and squabbled and often maimed one another. He decided to try a different strategy. Instead of selecting the chickens that individually produced the most eggs, he bred all the chickens in the communal *cages* that produced the most eggs. When he did that, the chickens' deadly skirmishes became quite infrequent. The individual animals might not have won any egg-production competitions, but because of their high level of social collaboration, they were able to maximize the egg-production ability they did have, and their descendants outproduced those of the individually excellent egg-layers. "They were not spending energy competing," explains Charles Goodnight, an evolutionary biologist at the University of Vermont. "By cooperating, the cage collectively produced more eggs."

While the theory of group selection is still controversial in the scientific world, it seems logical that how the members of a given society behave toward one another could make a difference to the reproductive prospects of each individual in the group. In human societies, for instance, when group members pitch in to help one another instead of acting completely selfishly, the overall survival rate of the group could potentially surpass that of a less-cooperative group, and each member's chances of passing on his or her genes would be higher. (Of course, groups of humans also compete against one another for resources—witness various world wars—so cooperation *within* groups does not mean an absence of competition *between* groups!)

Early populations of humans tended to travel in hunter-gatherer groups. Meat was one of their main food sources, and members of the group depended on one another to generously share their spoils so everyone could enjoy a steady food supply. They also relied on one another for protection from threats. The result? Group members reaped rewards that surpassed what any of them had to sacrifice individually. Any impulses certain members might have had to lord it over the others—and it's safe to say these impulses existed—were probably kept limited by their need for resources that the group alone could efficiently provide. "You look at humans and it looks like we are very group-selected," Goodnight says. "You put one person in the middle of the jungle and they're dinner. Twenty people, you have a village. We can't survive on our own, but we can collectively."

Evolutionary theories of altruism such as kin selection and group selection supply possible big-picture reasons why animals and humans have a substantial capacity for helping behavior. But these theories tell us little about the precise circuits within the brain that control these nurturing social impulses, which have long remained a mystery.

Using genes from sources such as algae and pond scum, the Stanford psychiatrist and bioengineer Karl Deisseroth has begun making headway on this question. Deisseroth is connecting the dots between neural circuits and social behaviors with the help of light-sensitive proteins found in nature. After incorporating the genes that code for such proteins into mouse neurons, Deisseroth can activate and deactivate the cells just by snaking an optical fiber into a mouse's brain and turning on the light.

Using this technique, Deisseroth demonstrated that it's possible to make mice more "prosocial"—in other words, more interested in other members of their species—than they might otherwise be. Like nearly all animals, mice can be bred with varying propensities to socialize and identify with other members of their species. "The two genes on the left show normal behavior. The mother will usually position herself over the pups to keep them warm," Deisseroth explains at a Stanford University conference, indicating a photo projected on a large screen. "On the right, the young pups are left on their own." He shows another picture, this one of young mice away from their mother—apparently the murine equivalent of a parent who plops her kids in front of the TV and heads to another room.

But those genetic predispositions can be overcome, at least to some degree, through neural manipulation. Deisseroth pulls up videos to illustrate. First, he shows a mouse that looks downright standoffish in the presence of one of its peers. "You can see that the larger animal is in fact running away from the smaller animal," he says. But in a later segment, light activates neurons in part of a mouse's brain known to help govern emotions like love in humans. Once the light in the mouse's brain begins to glow, the mouse all but smothers his cagemate, practically jumping on top of him in an attempt to connect.

Deisseroth's behavior-modifying technique might sound vaguely Orwellian, but he plans to use his light-activation system for benevolent ends. He aims to use it to figure out how mammals' brains govern their actions, which groups of neurons give rise to which behaviors. He's not looking to zap people's brains with light to force them to become more "prosocial" and attentive to others; he simply wants to understand where such generous behavior originates.

While Deisseroth explores the comprehensive underpinnings of the mammalian brain, the neuroscientist Jordan Grafman has investigated specific regions of the human brain that give rise to altruistic behavior. Grafman, now director of brain injury research at the Rehabilitation Institute of Chicago, is an imposing physical presence; he stands six feet tall and his voluminous white lab coat makes him appear even larger. But his laugh and low-key demeanor puts me at ease. I quickly pick up on the empathetic streak that's led him to pursue decades of neuroscience research with an eye toward helping brain-injured patients recover some function.

Grafman's interest in how the brain governs generosity arose in part out of his work with military veterans who suffered brain trauma. Back in the 1980s, when he was working with returned vets at Walter Reed Army Medical Center in Washington, D.C., he started to notice something unusual about patients who'd sustained damage to their frontal lobes. At first glance, they appeared normal: Their cognitive ability seemed unaffected, and many were able to carry out basic motor tasks with ease. But they suffered from other, more subtle deficits, many of which were apparent only in a nonclinical setting. "The wives said, 'You're missing something,'" Grafman remembers. In social situations, the men floundered, acting as if they didn't care what other people had to say.

Over the following years, Grafman's mind often wandered to the frontal-lobe-injured patients he'd treated who seemingly had limited capacity to identify with others. He hoped he would someday be able to investigate where empathy and generosity originated in the brain, and he got his best chance in the mid-2000s while working at the National Institutes of Health.

The advent of fMRI scanning, which highlighted the level of activity in different parts of the brain by measuring the amount of blood flow they received, made it much easier to see which parts of the brain were engaged as people carried out various tasks. To see if this tool could lend insight into the motivations behind giving behavior, Grafman and his colleagues recruited nineteen study subjects, placed each of them inside the fMRI scanner, and presented them with charities from a long list. For each charity, they could choose to donate money, refuse to donate money, or add money to a separate reward account that they could take home at the end of the study. (In some cases, it was especially costly for subjects to make a donation decision, because doing so required them to draw from their own reward accounts.) All the while, the scanner whirred in the background, recording the participants' brain activity.

The researchers weren't sure what to expect when they analyzed the study's results, but one day, Grafman's colleague Jorge Moll came up to him and said, "You're not going to believe this." The scans revealed that when people made the decision to donate to what they felt was a worthy organization, parts of the midbrain lit up—the same region that controls cravings for food and sex, and the same region that became active when the subjects added money to their personal reward accounts.

Gradually, Grafman began to realize how this finding made sense. While we often tend to think of altruism as a kind of sophisticated moral capacity we use to squelch our urges to dominate others, this new evidence suggests that giving is actually inherently rewarding: The brain churns out a pleasurable response when we engage in it.

But the subjects' high degree of midbrain activation wasn't the study's only interesting finding. Grafman points to a graphic on the giant computer monitor on his desk. "This is the subgenual area, part of the frontal lobes," he says, indicating a gumdrop-size region near the midpoint of the brain. The area contains lots of receptors for oxytocin, a hormone that promotes social bonding, and it was strongly active when his study subjects made the decision to give to charity. In a separate experiment by the Claremont Graduate University neuroeconomist Paul Zak, subjects given oxytocin were 80 percent more generous to strangers than subjects on a placebo. Findings like these indicate that altruism and social relationships are intimately connected—in part, it may be our reliance on the benefits of strong interpersonal connections that motivates us to behave unselfishly.

The experiment's altruism-feels-good finding was the one that got the most play in the press, but to Grafman, one of the most memorable results was what happened when subjects decided to make a donation even when they knew it was going to cost them money from their personal reward accounts. In these scenarios, a brain area called the anterior prefrontal cortex lit up—a region that's responsible for complex judgments and decision-making. These subjects were willing to give even when they knew it would cost them, indicating that this segment of the brain may help us decide to behave generously even when doing so runs counter to our immediate self-interest.

While he believes a multitude of brain areas work in concert to create unselfish behavior, Grafman views the anterior prefrontal cortex as the ultimate conductor of altruistic thoughts and actions. The prefrontal cortex generally regulates higher-level thought, but the anterior region is critical because it allows us to weigh a varied assortment of factors and predictions before deciding whether to give our time or money to a person or charitable cause. "This area is very important in looking at the future, in forecasting," Grafman says. "If you're donating, you're really thinking about how this organization is going to use the money you're giving. In many ways, that determines who you give to."

Grafman's work reveals that the prefrontal cortex is involved in making generous decisions, such as giving to charity or investing in a young student's education, that aren't necessarily going to have beneficial results until months or years down the line. It's also a part of the brain that helps us identify with others, a key prerequisite to taking unselfish action.

It makes sense, then, that when certain people sustain prefrontal cortex injuries, as some of Grafman's frontal-lobe patients did, they're less able to drum up empathy for others. The University of Wisconsin neuroscientist Michael Koenigs and his colleagues gathered patients who had sustained damage to the ventromedial region of the prefrontal cortex and asked them what they would do if they were in hiding with other people and their baby started crying, threatening to reveal the hideaways' location to enemy soldiers. These prefrontal-cortex-damaged subjects were more likely than noninjured participants to say they would suffocate the baby in order to keep the group's location secret. In a sense, their decision was entirely rational—so rational, in fact, that it would provoke most people to disgust. In other studies, too, people with damage to the prefrontal cortex show deficits in empathy, providing more evidence that—when fully functional—this region helps us formulate complex moral decisions about social matters like who and whether to help.

A part of the prefrontal cortex may also encourage unselfishness by giving us the capacity to understand how other people think, according to the Stanford psychologist Jamil Zaki. Zaki noticed that in games where players have the option to split an amount of money between themselves and someone else, they typically pay themselves more than they pay the other person—but rarely do they pay the other person nothing at all. "What jumps out at me," Zaki asks an audience of students and professors one afternoon on campus, "is why does the person not give zero on every trial?"

To investigate, Zaki devised a series of money-splitting scenarios to present to subjects when they were in an fMRI scanner, and in some of them, he asked them to speculate on the preferences of the partner they would be splitting with. He asked the subjects questions about the other person's likely habits and wishes, such as "Do you think this person would enjoy living in California?" When people engaged their medial prefrontal cortex more—an area involved in understanding others' thoughts—while thinking about their partners, they gave more generously to the partners later on.

This result underscores how important it is to develop empathy for someone else to lay the groundwork for extending aid to them. Zaki's finding hints that the brain mechanisms that allow us to understand other people's mental states also support our desire to help them—a tendency Zaki sees as innate and deep-rooted, emerging as naturally as any other aspect of human development. "Children, by one year of age, will spontaneously help others. It may be woven into our motivational system."

Woven into our motivational system, perhaps, but the weaving is by no means impeccable. While I'm impressed by the detail with which altruism researchers have traced the genesis of helping behavior in our brains and our ancestral environments, I can't stop thinking about all the times we don't come through for fellow humans—why, if we are in fact so hardwired to help and cooperate, we so frequently ignore one another's desperate circumstances. Why do we ignore the homeless man sitting on the curb, so desperately in need of a good meal and some kindness? Why do we shrink back from heroically defending moral principles we claim to believe in, like fairness and generosity? Why do I spend free weekend mornings lolling on the couch instead of lending a hand to people I know could really use it?

Where once there was only speculation about the origins of the human desire to help others, a body of data has whooshed in to fill the gap, revealing key workings of the biological hardware that makes altruism possible. This represents a new scientific frontier, one that could eventually enable the development of therapies tailored for people who have particular problems generating empathy or who want to improve their existing capacity for generosity. At the same time, theories about the evolution of altruism have expanded and acquired evidence to support them, lending insight into why our brains are wired for selflessness in the first place.

One problem with primarily biological explanations for generosity, though, is that they sometimes give short shrift to environmental influences and individual initiative. It's true enough that our genetics have evolved to include cooperative inclinations and create brain structures that predispose us to help, but the examples others set for us, the surroundings in which we live, and the values we most prize also play a significant role in tipping us toward selflessness or selfishness. In the end, what we do with our generous thoughts and inclinations is always up to us, much as what we do with our impulses to eat fatty food or cheat on our partners is up to us. "The biological isn't meant to explain everything," says the Georgetown University philosopher Judith Lichtenberg. "Kin selection doesn't explain why people do altruistic acts for strangers."

Maybe there's a more nuanced way to think about what Jakie did for Krom, then—a way that takes both biology and individual motivation into account. Jakie and Krom's ancestors may have lived in an environment where individuals' survival odds improved when they cooperated in a group setting, eventually boosting the prevalence of generosity genes in the population. So it's possible Jakie was genetically predisposed to help other members of his group, whether they were kin or not. Nevertheless, he could easily have ignored the impulse to help Krom and attended to his own immediate survival needs. He opted to devote his time to helping a group elder he respected, something other members of his group may not have chosen to do.

Likewise, biology alone cannot explain what motivates Anuradha Koirala to help scarred young Nepalese women build fulfilling lives. Certainly, there are any number of well-defined modules in her brain that may have compelled her to take action, and the fact that her ancestors evolved to live peaceably in small groups may have helped shape her outlook in fundamental ways. But in the end, Koirala's decision—like each decision we make about whether to take heroic or altruistic action—was unique and unrepeatable, a resolution that cannot be fully distilled into an evolved inheritance pattern or a burst of brain activity on an fMRI scanner. Scientific theories and measuring tools may help reveal the origins of generous impulses and the reasoning behind them, but each act of generosity remains shrouded in some essential degree of mystery.

While we are hardwired to "do unto others" in a multitude of ways, we also have power over whether to take advantage of those natural capacities or let them wither away unrealized. One promising way to strengthen these capacities may involve giving in strategic ways to reinforce the existing generosity pathways in our brains. As a result, we might not only be able to get hooked on self-sacrifice, but also be able to learn to love the entire process.

Chapter Two
THE ECONOMICS OF UNSELFISHNESS

Get in," the tech says. Gingerly, I swing my legs onto a narrow gurney-like platform and lie down. I stare at the ceiling as the tech plumps foam pads on either side of my skull, nestled around the industrial-strength ear protectors I'm wearing to block out the noise of the magnet. As I roll into the narrow tunnel of the machine, I take deep breaths to slow my pounding heart. Not only am I about to undergo the first MRI scan of my life, I'm about to take part in an experiment that will reveal whether my brain fits the profile of a selfish person's or a generous one's.

Classical economic theory holds that humans are basically self-interested: Given the choice, we'll often opt for a personal benefit over a personal loss, even if that loss involves a benefit to someone else. The well-known philosopher and economist John Stuart Mill championed the self-centered theory in the mid-1800s, describing man as a creature that "does that by which he may obtain the greatest amount of necessaries, conveniences and luxuries, with the smallest quantity of labor and physical self-denial."

These days, the reign of Wall Street titans might seem to prove that personal acquisition is the overriding motivation for human behavior, but the broader world supplies ample evidence that this I-me-mine credo is an oversimplification. In actuality, most people show great generosity—even heroic generosity—in some circumstances and great selfishness in others. So what rational calculations play into the giving choices we ultimately make? Can being generous ever truly make economic sense?

Bill Harbaugh has devoted countless hours to addressing these kinds of questions. The University of Oregon economist exudes an offbeat charm that belies the seriousness of his work—his website identifies him as "Bill Harbaugh A.K.A.: Billy Harbaugh, W. T. Harbaugh, William Harbaugh, William T. Harbaugh, Herr Doctor Professor William Talbot Harbaugh, Ph.D." He's also curator of the Museum of Scientifically Accurate Fabric Brain Art, a collection that currently contains, among other things, a wall-size rug his wife created that depicts slices of the brain in cross-section. After going on sabbatical in Aix-en-Provence, he used Mathematica software to illustrate how many kisses it would take for every person in his daughter's French school class to greet one another, as tradition required. (The final tally, assuming a class of 30 people: 435 kisses.)

While Harbaugh has made his name as an economist, he has the instincts of a psychologist—an observer obsessed with what people choose to do and why. He first became interested in charitable giving because it seemed like an intriguing exception to the rule that most people will act in their direct self-interest. "It seems odd that people give money away," he says, chuckling. But we *do* give, consistently and in large amounts. In 2011, Americans gave a staggering $298.3 billion to charity—a 3.9 percent increase over the previous year, and more than the entire gross domestic product of many nations.

Giving is catnip to social scientists like Harbaugh because it shatters the conventional wisdom that we're motivated mainly to secure maximum resources for ourselves and our kin. But canonical studies in the field have suggested that maximizing personal gain isn't necessarily the primary goal under all circumstances. Back in the 1970s, for instance, the Cornell psychology student William Upton had a recruiter contact two groups of potential donors at Denver and Kansas City blood banks. The first group received a simple, standard call to donate at an upcoming blood drive, while the second group was offered a ten-dollar reward if they gave blood at the drive. Principles of economic self-interest dictated that more would-be donors would turn out for a monetary reward than for nothing, but the opposite happened. Among highly motivated donors, those who were promised cash were actually *less* likely to respond to the request and donate to the drive. The cash reward, then, apparently served as a *dis*incentive to donate, suggesting that some people donated to blood banks because helping with no strings attached was rewarding in itself. When a monetary reward was offered, the scenario became more transactional than altruistic—perhaps people who received the reward-based appeal felt that donating blood wasn't *really* a helpful act if they were receiving cash in return.

Harbaugh's own early look at givers' motivations, though, reinforced the more traditional view that people give because they expect some tangible reward—if not a monetary one, then a social one. In the late 1990s, he studied a group of law school graduates donating to their alma mater; the institution grouped them into different donation brackets, entitling them to varying levels of recognition in public alumni giving reports. A donor who gave $500 or above, for example, was placed in a higher bracket than someone who gave only $450, and donors who gave $1,000 or more were placed in a higher bracket still. Harbaugh wasn't all that surprised when alumni donations clustered at the lowest end of each bracket, indicating people were giving just enough to be in the highest public tier accessible to them and little more. "People care about prestige," he says.

Do people sacrifice valuable goods for others—anything from their discretionary income to, in extreme cases, their health or safety—because they expect something in return? Do they give because it supplies a brain buzz? Or do they just enjoy the knowledge that they're helping someone else? The University of California, Berkeley, sociologist Robb Willer doesn't see the answers as straightforward—we're not completely selfish in our giving habits, but we're not purely altruistic, either. "People take on great risks to help others. They exhibit clear signs of joy when they see someone enjoys a gift," he says. "But on the other hand, we have all this evidence that giving is totally strategic. People will give way less money if they don't think anyone's going to know about their charitable donation. If you're dining with others, you're going to tip more than if you're dining alone. How do you reconcile this?"

Harbaugh set out to pinpoint exactly what is going on in people's brains when they decide to give to someone else. He sensed, though, that he wouldn't be able to assess people's motives accurately by asking them about their reasons for giving. He knew they'd tend to admit only the most innocuous reasons: that they felt sorry for the recipient, maybe, or that they just felt moved to help them out. No one would ever say, "I gave so I could impress other people," even if it were true. So Harbaugh aimed to shine a light on people's internal giving calculations without running headlong into their natural ego defenses.

In talks with his psychologist colleague Ulrich Mayr, he hit on a solution. The two of them would round up some interview subjects and put them in an fMRI scanner to take a close look at the blood flow in their brains. "Using the scanner, you could get at people's preferences without having to ask them," Mayr says. While subjects were in the scanner, a computer monitor in front of them would present them with opportunities to donate from a fund of $100 in real cash they'd received at the beginning of the experiment. The suggested donations could be as low as $15 or as high as $45. The subjects' donation decisions had meaning, since they would get to pocket whatever money was left over—if they gave away most of it, they'd have little to take home, and if they kept it all, they'd leave with a nice chunk of change.

As the subjects contemplated whether and how much to give to a food bank, the fMRI scanner would remain at work, recording what areas of the brain were activated at different points in the experiment. Harbaugh also opted to add another wrinkle: Some of the donations would be "voluntary," meaning the subjects would get to decide whether or not to give to charity, and some would be "involuntary," meaning the computer would simply inform the subjects that they were required to give a certain amount—a condition similar to real-life taxation.

After the experiment, Harbaugh and Mayr scrutinized the fMRI data to see which areas of the brain lit up in response to various giving scenarios. Some of their results tallied with basic Econ 101 principles—for instance, people were more likely to help the charity when the suggested contribution was relatively low. Other findings, however, were more surprising. When subjects decided to give to charity, areas of the brain associated with the processing of unexpected rewards, such as the nucleus accumbens, lit up. The nucleus accumbens, which releases the pleasure chemical dopamine, "is almost like the common currency of the brain. It keeps track of rewards, whatever kind they are," Harbaugh says. "There's some primary reward people get from seeing money go from themselves to provide to other people." His results tallied with the researcher Jordan Grafman's fMRI experiments showing pleasurable activation in the midbrain during giving. Harbaugh's study indicated that giving to charity is, surprisingly, neurologically similar to ingesting an addictive drug or learning you've received a winning lottery ticket.

It seems clear, then, that people give to charity not only because they think it's a good thing to do but also because giving makes them feel good, in addition to the particular benefit they're bestowing on the recipient. Even when subjects in Harbaugh's study were *required* to donate, this pleasurable response persisted, though it was not as strong as when people got to choose whether to donate on their own. Harbaugh thinks his results offer a decent argument for taxing people to raise money to benefit the needy, since people being taxed actually *do* get satisfaction from giving a mandatory gift. Taxation also makes sense, he says, because we sometimes need a nudge in order to take generous action, even if we have real empathy for the people we're helping. "You can be genuinely altruistic, feel good about other people being helped, but that does not necessarily move you to action, because of the tendency to free ride. The thing that would really make society stick together is this mutual agreement to rely on coercion—you want a society where everyone volunteers, but it's not a way to get roads and hospitals built." (It's possible that the "coerced satisfaction" people get from paying taxes in real life would be enhanced if they knew exactly what causes their tax dollars were supporting.)

Since some of Harbaugh's subjects showed more nucleus accumbens activation than others when they thought about seeing their money go to charity, he figured they were probably experiencing vastly different levels of satisfaction as a result. He divided the subjects into two groups: "egoists," who showed less nucleus accumbens activity at the prospect of seeing their money go to charity, and "altruists," who showed much more. In general, the greater the pleasurable brain activation, the more likely subjects were to give frequently, supporting the existence of a relationship between the wiring of our neural reward mechanism and our propensity to donate. "You can actually measure how much activation there is and predict with some degree of accuracy how much they're going to give," Harbaugh says. That individual variation in how people's brains reward them for giving could help explain why some people donate huge chunks of their paycheck to charitable causes year after year, while others prefer to hoard almost everything they earn.

On the other hand, there were a few outliers in Harbaugh's experiment: people who fit squarely in the "egoist" category from a biological perspective, but who donated at rates that surpassed what the nucleus accumbens activation on their scans would predict. These people, you could argue, were actually the most dedicated altruists: they were willing to give because they knew it would help others, even if giving didn't make them feel all that great. Harbaugh has since expanded on his initial experiment, looking at factors like whether or not people are more likely to give if someone else is watching. (Unsurprisingly, we *are* more generous when we think people are looking, which is probably why operas and ballet companies take great pains to list the names of donors in the back of programs.)

On balance, Harbaugh's work suggests that giving completely for its own sake—with absolutely *zero* expectation of pleasure or other reward in return—is rare. We're forever making complex calculations about whether or not to give in different situations, but whether or not our gift will help someone is far from the only factor we consider. The better we feel when we give, in general, the more often we do it. And as the Georgetown philosopher Judith Lichtenberg points out, even when we *think* we're giving with absolutely no expectation of reward, we can't be sure; our motivations (feeling good? looking good? gaining social leverage?) may be unconscious, inaccessible even to ourselves. "It's a very intractable question," she says. "No matter how altruistic a person is, you can say there's always some motive lurking." In other words, the widespread theory that altruists—even Mother Teresa–

caliber ones—have some selfish motivation cannot really be proven wrong. (Hence one of the most common responses I got from people who learned I was working on this book: "You know there's no such thing as true altruism, right?")

But the notion that real-world altruism is typically a sophisticated form of exchange or a reward-based proposition, rather than a no-strings-attached giving venture, doesn't bother Harbaugh all that much. His take on altruism is an eminently practical one: While there may be meaningful moral differences among the woman who gives because it makes her feel good, the one who does so because she expects kudos in return, and the one who does so only because the government requires her to, the net benefit to society is more or less the same. (Givers who outright manipulate potential recipients, however, transgress an important moral boundary—as, for instance, when a benefactor makes a college tuition gift contingent on choosing an unwanted course of study. Desiring recognition for your contribution or feeling good about it is one thing; insisting upon a predefined outcome is another.)

When Harbaugh talked with the Dalai Lama a few years ago, he was surprised at how closely the Buddhist leader's take on unselfishness matched his own. "I thought he had a very pragmatic view of altruism—it was a constrained view. The question came up, 'If you use incentives to encourage people to behave more altruistically, is that genuine altruism?' His reaction was sort of, 'Whatever works.'" Insisting upon altruism with no expectation of accompanying pleasure or reward does seem too strict, a sort of hair-shirt, crawling-through-the-labyrinth vision of morality. What does it matter, after all, whether or not we feel good while we perform a generous act, as long as the act gets done?

Still, the notion that giving is meaningful even if givers' motives are less than pure remains anathema to some. In her memoir, *Dream*

Catcher, Peggy Salinger—daughter of J. D. Salinger, author of *The Catcher in the Rye*—writes about how her father reacted after she signed up for a hospital chaplaincy internship, consoling patients in the midst of medical crises. The elder Salinger asked his daughter whether she struggled with her ego doing chaplaincy work. Wasn't the whole thing just vanity—doing something that appeared unselfish in order to feel "holier-than-thou" and look good to the world?

In the face of her father's criticism, Peggy Salinger ultimately decided that as long as she was helping someone else, it didn't really matter if her motives were less than saintly. "I just can't see worrying over one's motivations," she wrote, "with the single-minded absorption of an adolescent going at his pimples in the mirror."

As the walls of the scanner close in around my head, I will myself to relax, but I can't keep my shoulders from tensing up. I know the magnet in the machine is so strong that it could move metal around inside my body, and though I signed forms beforehand to verify I didn't have any pacemakers or other metal implants, I'm still paranoid about the possibility of my insides getting rearranged. The MRI tech told me it was OK to keep my bra on during the experiment, but it's a little disconcerting to feel the underwires tugging around my rib cage as the magnet encircling my head draws them toward it.

Like other subjects in Harbaugh's recent studies, I'm presented with descriptions of a diverse assortment of charities as I lie in the fMRI scanner. Once I've read each description, the computer screen overhead presents me with a potential donation scenario—for instance, the charity might get $20 in one scenario, while in another scenario, it might get only $10. I have a few seconds to decide whether to accept the proposed transfer, then I indicate my choice with a clicker device that's resting on my stomach. After every transfer, the program asks me how much I liked the transaction, on a scale of 1 to 4.

As I navigate through the questions and make my giving deci-sions, the scanner whines in the background like a band saw, so loud I can hear it clearly through the earplugs and ear protectors. About halfway through the experiment, I get a break from questions so the machine can do an in-depth structural scan of my brain. After my session in the scanner, I finally get up from the platform, dazed, test-ing my limbs to make sure they still work.

Harbaugh promises to get back to me with the results of my brain scans as soon as he's had a chance to analyze them. As I think about what I might possibly learn about myself, I get a little nervous. What if my brain's workings reveal I'm fundamentally stingy at my core—or, at least, somewhere in the vicinity of my nucleus accumbens?

It takes a few months for Harbaugh to finish his full analysis, but in the meantime, he sends me some high-resolution black-and-white images of my brain. "You have these three views here, sagittal, coronal, axial," he says as I scrutinize the cross-sectional contents of my skull. Displayed on my laptop screen, my head's innards look a little like a stalk of cauliflower cut in half lengthwise. The white stuff I see is the brain's inner wiring, networks of neurons connected to one another, while the butterfly wing–shaped gaps on either side of this white mat-ter are ventricles, which contain cushioning fluid.

The next time Harbaugh and I see each other, he's ready to show me more. He clicks over to a window on his computer screen showing my brain in cross section, but these images aren't pure black and white like the first set of pictures I saw. Instead, there are red splotches in many different areas, making the screen glow like a Lite-Brite display. Harbaugh explains that he ran a computer analysis looking for pat-terns of activation in the brain as I was navigating through the dona-tion scenarios; areas that are more activated than the rest, as evidenced by increased blood flow, are highlighted in red. "It's kind of cool because instead of a bunch of random noise, the areas that are activated are ones that are very sensible," he continues. "This splotch up here, the anterior cingulate cortex, that's an area that activates in any kind of decision task. The fact it's activating is like proof of concept. The dorsolateral prefrontal cortex—this area definitely has connections to the dopaminergic system, so it's reasonable that those areas are activated."

I listen attentively as Harbaugh explains the blood-flow patterns in various areas of my brain, but I can hardly wait to ask the one question that's been on my mind ever since I stepped out of the scanner in Oregon. "In your study, you classified people as egoists or altruists based on the brain activation patterns you saw. Where do you think I would fall on that scale?"

Harbaugh smiles. "If I'm right, you're showing more activation in the dopaminergic areas when you're seeing the charity getting money than when you're getting money for yourself. You're definitely showing activation that is consistent with the altruist. You are getting neural benefit from knowing people are doing better."

I exhale a long breath. I've been convinced Harbaugh's scans will unmask me as an innately selfish person, one whose brain recoils at the thought of giving (which I still feel like I am, sometimes). It's a relief to know that's probably not the case. To help explain my results, Harbaugh shows me a graph that plots the amount of pleasurable brain activation subjects showed against the amount they actually gave to charity during the study. "For *you*, you liked to give and you gave. That's no mystery," Harbaugh says. "The people who are on this line"—he indicates a slash running diagonally through the field of dots—"their behavior is very consistent with rational choice." In other words, like me, they felt good when they gave, so they gave fairly generously. But Harbaugh points out that the rewarding activation some other subjects' brains showed during giving scenarios *wasn't* accompanied by large charitable contributions. "They should have given, but they made a mistake by not giving."

I like knowing that my brain gets happy when I donate, and that knowledge, I hope, will help convince me to keep giving in the future, pushing past the initial hesitation I often feel at giving away money or time. I wonder what would happen if more people could get their brains scanned, could be presented with evidence that being generous gives them real satisfaction. Would it compel them to donate more? More broadly, does Harbaugh's work point to strategies that could be tried to encourage people to give more generously overall, an essential skill for people working on a more heroic approach to life? Could we maximize the pleasure we get from giving to such an extent that we naturally start to crave it?

When I raise these questions with Harbaugh, he seems a little bemused that I'm asking. "You can change your taste for all kinds of things. Of course there's a possibility you could get people to change their behavior. It would be astonishing if there weren't." Research on conditioning and reinforcement shows the importance of the brain's reward circuitry, including the nucleus accumbens, in instilling desired behaviors. "When you do something that triggers the dopaminergic system in the brain," he says, "you want to do it again." Working from this principle, Harbaugh envisions some straightforward potential ways to reinforce generosity. If charities ask donors for relatively small amounts of money to start with, for example, the neural reward that comes with giving will more likely outweigh the pain of giving up money. Having had a pleasurable experience on balance, donors might be more apt to return to give. Behavioral studies of volunteers, in fact, indicate that something similar may be happening when people decide to give their time to someone else—the more often they volunteer, the more likely they are to do it again. Strangely enough, then, selflessness can grow from impulses that are essentially self-centered.

Can we get ourselves addicted to doing good by giving modest amounts of money or time on a regular basis, exercising the pathways in our brain that allow us to derive pleasure from generosity? It may be a winning proposition for the brain and its owner, as well as for the world at large. And if Stanford's Phil Zimbardo is right, such consistent selflessness priming may prepare us to seize opportunities to perform larger heroic deeds if and when they arise. Given what scientists now know—that many people's brains are wired in certain ways to enjoy helping others—not to exercise that generous wiring in real life seems, well, selfish.

But even when we take optimistic brain studies like Harbaugh's and Grafman's into account, it's hard to deny that there are plenty of cases where people circumvent their generous wiring or work against it. Biology and neurology have recorded many instances of apparently hardwired generosity, like Harbaugh's observation that the pleasure centers of our brain light up when we support a good cause. Still, there are just as many instances where our altruistic impulses fail spectacularly, where we fail to intervene heroically: children going hungry by the hundreds of thousands, throngs of poor people on the streets who no one seems to see, large-scale genocides like the one in Rwanda. When things like this happen, most of us do little or nothing to remedy the situation. I think uncomfortably of the times when I saw some kid getting bullied and steered clear of trying to stop it, or when I chose to sleep in rather than attending a volunteer group meeting. So how can generosity coexist alongside callous disregard for others—two warring impulses generated within the same human brain? What holds us back from attaining our full selflessness potential?

Chapter Three
MENTAL BLOCKS AGAINST HEROISM

F lash back nearly seventy years to 1944. A young Jewish girl named Anne Frank was hiding with her family in the spare rooms behind her father's offices in Amsterdam, the Netherlands. Dozens of her Jewish friends had already been deported to unknown destinations, and she'd heard reports on Allied radio that the deportees were being killed with gas. She kept a diary in which she recorded her hopes, fears, and observations of the world around her. By late summer, she and her family would be arrested and sent to Westerbork concentration camp to join thousands of other Dutch Jews slated for deportation to Auschwitz.

Nearly fifty years later, Zlata Filipović, a young Bosnian girl, would begin keeping a similar diary. She wrote about how she couldn't concentrate on her homework when she heard gunfire coming from the hills. She wrote about how a group of armed civilians crashed a wedding, killing a Serbian guest and injuring the priest. Her diary chronicled life inside a war in which 100,000 of her fellow Bosnian citizens were killed and 2.2 million were displaced.

The two young writers' stories ended differently. Anne died of typhus—alone and unnoticed by the world—at Bergen-Belsen concentration camp in 1945, while Zlata survived, escaping to Paris with her family in 1993. But in both cases, their writing enabled an important kind of alchemy. The notebooks and loose sheets of Anne's diary, which Miep Gies gathered from the floor of the Frank family's hiding place after their arrest, would eventually be published by Doubleday under the title *The Diary of a Young Girl*, and the words Zlata penned became *Zlata's Diary: A Child's Life in Sarajevo*. The vivacity and clarity of the diaries' descriptions enabled readers to understand exactly what the writers had gone through: the pain, heartbreak, and uncertainty they'd felt as they contemplated their own possible death, the joy they felt when they concluded, in fleeting moments, that maybe there was hope for humanity after all.

The two once-anonymous diarists became international sensations, one posthumously, the other in life. (In a tribute to Anne, who called her diary "Kitty," Zlata dubbed hers "Mimmy.") To date, Anne's book has sold more than 25 million copies, and many museum exhibits have been erected in her honor. Zlata has been toasted by leaders around the world and is given a hero's welcome wherever she goes. Now a filmmaker, speaker, and social activist, she has entered into collaborations with the Anne Frank House, UNICEF, and the United Nations.

Anne's and Zlata's stories raise an important question. Why are we so willing to anoint these two young diarists as celebrities, to sympathize with every adolescent concern and worry that appears on the page, in Anne's case to dedicate whole *museum exhibits* to them—while at the same time remaining utterly unresponsive to the plight of other victims in similar situations? American newspapers printed reports of atrocities and Jewish massacres before the end of World War II, when the bloodshed still could have been halted or slowed, but the United States government chose not to initiate military strikes against death camps such as Auschwitz. Similarly, the United States had knowledge of what was happening in Bosnia but did not intervene decisively enough to prevent mass killing.

Today many people continue to be killed in conflict zones around the world and in violence-ridden neighborhoods in the United States, but there is very little outcry. It's all too easy to read the number-crammed news blurbs, often no more than a few paragraphs long, and feel singularly apathetic, even though we know in theory that the number 200,000 represents the end of 200,000 lives just as valuable as those of Zlata or Anne Frank. Why do we embrace known victims like Anne and Zlata with open arms, but act as if nameless, faceless victims who suffer just as intensely do not even exist? More generally, why do we strive to help someone in our neighborhood or church out of a tight spot, but fail to extend ourselves similarly for someone in equally urgent need whom we do not know? Why do we click off the TV with scarcely a second thought when we hear stories about thousands of high school dropouts or poor children who are hungry? The answers are critical, because these human tendencies present a problem for those who aim to help us fulfill our full altruistic and heroic potential.

The Polish poet Wisława Szymborska once wrote, "My imagination . . . doesn't cope well with big numbers. It's still moved by singularity." Our inclination to focus strongly on the particular is one reason we sometimes fail to take unselfish action. "People are willing to do so much to save individuals, but they fail to respond when the numbers are large," says the psychologist Paul Slovic. "After the Holocaust, we said 'never again,' but that has become 'again and again.'"

Slovic is the president of Decision Research in Eugene, Oregon, a city where small throngs of homeless teens and adults wander against a backdrop of lush foliage and impeccably kept Craftsman homes. He greets me in his charmingly disorganized second-floor office space, the shelves crammed full of books angled in every direction; the perpetual half smile on his face appears ready to break into a grin at any moment. His area of interest, he explains to me, is why people decide to do what they do—a topic that's supplied enough research material to keep him busy for several lifetimes.

Slovic has been interested in what motivates people's decision-making since the late 1950s. At one point, he carried out seemingly innocuous research showing that people's impressions of a given location (California as relaxed beach country, for instance, or Las Vegas as a den of sin) played a critical role in determining how likely they were to move or retire to those locations. In retrospect, he came to see this work as a key demonstration of just how strongly people's initial feelings about a situation predict their subsequent behavior.

When the Darfur genocides started to ramp up in the mid-2000s, Slovic was stunned at how—despite reports about thousands of dying, including young children and babies—individual countries, and humanity more generally, were failing to stop the slaughter. Years ago, Slovic had attended a moving lecture where Elie Wiesel, a Nobel Peace Prize winner and author of the best-selling Holocaust memoir *Night*, spoke about humanity's indifference to genocide. He read Samantha Power's *A Problem from Hell*, a grim chronicle of the U.S. government's failures to take action in the face of mass atrocities.

The ever-present problem of genocides that no one bothered to stop got Slovic thinking about the Princeton emeritus psychologist Daniel Kahneman's so-called prospect theory. The theory essentially states that when stimuli get more intense, changes are harder to detect. Most people can readily pick up the difference between whispering and normal conversation volume, for example, but the intensity difference between a vacuum's whine and a jet engine's roar is harder to detect. Similarly, it's easy for us to see the visual difference between a group of 5 people and a group of 10, but much harder to see the difference between a group of 95 and a group of 100. The same goes for the value we ascribe to things. "Value increases in a nonlinear way. The interesting thing is how it flattens out," Slovic says. "If you gain a hundred dollars, you get some value, but if you go to two hundred, the subjective satisfaction you get is something less than twice what you get from one hundred."

Slovic wondered if this phenomenon might help explain why people were reluctant to take action to help large groups of others—they might have trouble truly comprehending the difference between 200 victims and 2,000, and therefore not feel an urgent need to act. He and his colleagues came up with a hypothetical scenario. They told experimental participants a story about a grant-funding agency and asked for their judgment as to how many lives a medical institute should have to save before being worthy of a $10 million grant. When subjects were told there were 15,000 people whose lives were at risk, they stated that about 9,000 lives would need to be saved to make the grant worthwhile, in effect making each life worth just over $1,100. When subjects were told that 290,000 people's lives were at risk, however, they said the grant should be given if there was potential to save 100,000 lives, making each life worth about $100. In other words, people saw 9,000 lives that were part of a smaller population as equal in value to *100,000* lives that were part of a larger population.

Another scenario asked participants to imagine they were government officials deciding whether to support programs designed to provide clean water to Rwandan refugees at a camp in Zaire. The programs, they were told, would save 4,500 lives. People generally perceived the intervention as *less* worthy when the stated size of the camp's refugee population increased from 11,000 to 250,000, even though they would have been saving the same number of lives each time.

What all this means is that we don't typically interpret the value of a life as constant—we see it as highly variable, dependent on the sheer number of other victims in the picture. "An individual life is very valuable when it is considered singly, but we feel little different about the prospect of eighty-eight deaths than we do eighty-seven," Slovic says. He knew he'd hit on something important: When large numbers were involved, people seemed to lose sight of the absolute value of each individual life.

To find out how people responded to the plight of individuals as opposed to large groups, Slovic designed a study with Deborah Small of the University of Pennsylvania and George Loewenstein at Carnegie Mellon University. Some participants in the study were given $5 and were introduced to an imaginary seven-year-old child named Rokia, who they were told was in severe need of food aid. They were shown a picture of Rokia, who had large eyes and a solemn expression, and were asked if they wanted to donate money to help relieve the child's hunger. Others were supplied with the same $5, heard a more generalized story about millions of starving Africans, and were asked to donate the money to help them all. The final group heard Rokia's story and were also supplied with the same statistics as the second group.

The difference between the first two groups was stark. The donors who were introduced to Rokia on her own gave her nearly half of the $5 they had been allotted, almost $2.50, but the group presented only with the impersonal statistics about starvation gave much less—just over a dollar. The most baffling finding, though, was that the donors presented with both Rokia's story *and* the starvation statistics didn't donate much more than a dollar, either. That suggested the statistics actually had some kind of dampening effect on people's feelings for Rokia, causing them to give much less than they would have if they had encountered her story on its own.

Slovic wondered what would happen if people had the choice to give to one child or a *small* group of children. He was familiar with the work of the Israeli researchers Tehila Kogut and Ilana Ritov, who supplied certain subjects with children's names, ages, and pictures, then asked some of these participants whether they would donate money so one child could have a life-saving medical treatment and asked others whether they'd donate so a group of eight children could all have the same treatment. People expressed greater willingness to help the single identified child, despite the opportunity to help a larger number of children by donating to the group.

To see if this generosity-dilution effect held true for groups as small as two people, Slovic and his colleagues came up with another set of Rokia scenarios. Some subjects heard the heart-wrenching story of Rokia, and others heard the story of her friend Moussa, who was said to be living in equally dire conditions. A third group heard about both Rokia *and* Moussa. After hearing the stories, subjects were given the opportunity to donate. The results confirmed what Slovic had suspected based on the Israeli study: People were significantly more likely to give to only one needy child than to two at a time. "It wasn't as huge a difference as one [child] versus eight," Slovic says, "but their feelings of sympathy and compassion dropped."

The University of North Carolina psychologists Daryl Cameron and Keith Payne refer to this predictable phenomenon as the collapse of compassion. The two researchers asked subjects to read a story about victims of violence in Darfur and then gauged their emotional reactions to the story and accompanying pictures. When subjects were asked to donate money to help the child or children pictured, they displayed less compassion toward a group of eight children than toward a single child, indicating that their capacity for compassion eroded as the numbers rose and as they sensed more would be expected of them. (Interestingly, when subjects were *not* asked to give money, they reported feeling more compassion for the larger group of eight children.) In a follow-up experiment, Cameron and Payne found that subjects identified as "skilled emotional regulators"—people who are good at controlling their emotions—are most likely to succumb to the collapse of compassion.

Whether consciously or unconsciously, we may modulate our compassion levels based on how capable we feel of improving the situation at hand. If parents tell a teacher that their child is being bullied on the playground, for example, the teacher can take concrete steps to resolve the problem: keeping a closer eye on the alleged perpetrators, or assigning them detention if they act out. If that same teacher reads a newspaper account about thousands of starving children in Somalia or mass violence in Darfur, she's more apt to close the paper with a sigh, feeling that since there's nothing concrete she can do about the problem, she's not going to let her emotions get the best of her. "Probably at least sometimes people don't know they're doing it," Payne says. "Like when you're flipping channels and you come across one of these ads for Save the Children—most people's reaction is just to flip the channel."

What's striking is that people's actual behavior in experimental situations diverges so sharply from what their moral code tells them they should do. Ask people whether every human life is of equal dignity, and most of them will say yes; this principle of basic human equality is even codified in the UN's Universal Declaration of Human Rights. Yet when we have a chance to help two children instead of one—and theoretically do more good—we tend to falter.

Why do we behave in ways that don't conform to our own most strongly held ethical principles? More specifically, why do we hang back just when we have a chance to extend our altruistic reach by helping multiple people? Slovic thinks part of the answer might lie in our evolutionary origins. When predators were around every corner, people capable of making snap moral judgments without thinking about the implications may have had a survival advantage. "It may have been very adaptive in the face of danger," Slovic says. "We *can* step back, say 'Let me think harder,' and come up with some logical response, but we usually don't do that." Instead, we tend to go with our gut reaction, which may not be in line with our morals. And during most of human history, Slovic points out, there was no need for us to know or care about what was going on at a distance. That could explain why our brains are not strongly adapted to alert us to take action in situations we cannot witness firsthand, such as mass starvation in India or Somalia.

But another Cameron and Payne study hints at a way aspiring heroes or altruists can overcome the tendency to tune out when they learn about groups of people who need help. When participants in this study were told to distance themselves from their emotions, they limited their compassion. But when they were specifically told to let themselves feel their emotions without trying to get rid of them, they did not show any such signs of compassion collapse.

One way of escaping compassion-numbing effects, then, may be to give yourself explicit permission to feel. If you see a throng of homeless people sitting on the sidewalk, instead of walking right past without slowing down, you can tell yourself it's all right to feel an empathetic pang—and maybe even hand over your lunch leftovers to one of them. This perception change doesn't just involve a onetime mental shift, though; it takes sustained, deliberate effort. And it's no small matter to find the right balance between being generous and overextending yourself in an effort to solve other people's problems—an emotional pitfall the collapse of compassion may have arisen to prevent.

More and more, charitable organizations have started heeding psychological principles similar to those Slovic, Cameron, and Payne describe while developing donation campaigns. In lieu of bombarding people with off-the-charts statistics about poverty, homelessness, and ethnic cleansing, these outfits are churning out promotional materials that feature the names, faces, and stories of individuals—all in a concerted effort to awaken people's empathetic responses. The San Francisco–based nonprofit Kiva stands out for its skill at harnessing the human tendency to focus on individuals instead of overwhelming statistics. Microfinancing organizations, which parcel out loans to small businesses to help them get off the ground, have been staples of startup business practice in the Third World for some time, but Kiva ups the ante by seeking to forge a direct personal connection between lenders and the people they're lending to.

The front page of the Kiva website is a collage of portrait photographs. When you click on one, you're presented with stories of individual would-be entrepreneurs, rounded out with additional information about their everyday lives. "Maweu is 45 years old, married and has three children," one story begins. "He repairs shoes to earn a living. He has been in this business for 14 years. Maweu describes his business environment as good because of limited competition. . . . He hopes to open a shoe shop and be financially stable." After reading Maweu's story, potential donors have a chance to finance a loan along with other contributors to help him buy sewing thread and shoe soles. Another aspiring entrepreneur, Leliosa, age thirty-five, lives in the Philippines with her husband and son and runs a tool-selling stand in a mall. "Through all her hard work on her business, Leliosa wants to expand her store and to help her child finish his schooling," the blurb reads. Since its inception, Kiva has supplied entrepreneurs from all over the world with more than $384 million in loans, supplied by more than 850,000 donors. The average Kiva user has made more than nine loans.

In addition, influential members of the media have taken note of the newest research. After learning about Slovic's work, the columnist

Nicholas Kristof decided to punctuate his writings about big issues such as conflict and genocide with personal stories in an attempt to elicit greater compassion and understanding in his readers. "My job as a journalist is to find these larger issues that I want to address but then find some microcosm of it, some Rokia who can open those portals and hopefully get people to care," he told the journalist Krista Tippett in 2010.

But while the implications of studies like Slovic's may be obvious to pundits and nonprofits that have a vested interest in eliciting a particular response from followers, the takeaway for people who want to surmount their *own* tendencies toward tuning out suffering is less clear. This is a very personal issue for me; I see signs of my own compassion collapse every time I hang up on a caller soliciting money for the hungry, every time I grow overwhelmed by the mere thought of making headway against vast societal problems such as urban poverty or the school-dropout epidemic. So how do we do it, I ask Slovic—how do we get past our own tendency to shut down so we can help the people who truly need it? He smiles, leans back in his chair. "That's the question," he says. "How do we deal with this?"

While Slovic doesn't claim to have all the answers, he's come to believe that the more you can infuse your perception of a dire situation with what Wisława Szymborska calls "singularity," the more likely you are to take action to help. So one potential way to push your numbness aside is to find your own Rokia—someone you can connect with on a personal level. People who heard her tragic story donated more money than people who heard an impersonal litany of starvation statistics in part because they felt they *knew* Rokia. She wasn't a faceless statistic; she was a real person in need of help. This is also why Anne Frank's and Zlata Filipović's diaries were so important in helping people wrap their minds around large-scale tragedies like the Holocaust and the war in Bosnia: They brought home the magnitude of suffering that individuals had endured. Similarly, to bring large-scale social issues home to yourself, to lend them singularity, you could respond to a litany of grim statistics in the paper ("Of all the socioeconomically disadvantaged high school students in California, 17.7 percent quit school before graduating. . . .") by serving as an after-school tutor, getting to know individual kids and their struggles—and in the process, getting a real-world look at the consequences of poverty and educational inequality. Teachers looking to sharpen their students' empathetic instincts might try telling the stories of large-scale genocides, wars, and social struggles through the stories of individual people who experienced them: Elie Wiesel, Cesar Chavez, Nelson Mandela, and others. An important part of overcoming the numbness large numbers induce involves creating the ideal conditions in which *other* people's most altruistic impulses can emerge.

Once we realize our brains are ill equipped to process the plight of thousands or millions, we can consciously avoid succumbing to our emotionless reactions to large-scale tragedies. Slovic recommends that would-be altruists teach themselves to rely on morally grounded logical reasoning instead. Learning that a thousand women and children were killed in a civil war, for instance, may not bring on a flood of tears, but when we pause and take a few minutes to process the true extent of what has happened, we'll conclude that we need to take immediate and decisive action to prevent more innocents from being hurt.

With awareness and practice, we can turn our strong empathetic bias toward individuals into a strength rather than a weakness, using stories like Rokia's as a conduit to greater, more profound understanding of the planet's problems. Deliberately seeking to understand large-scale tragedies or social inequities on a human level is one way of bringing them into our immediate vicinity, motivating us to do something about them—and giving us valuable information about the strategies that are most likely to be effective. This kind of personalization is also an ideal way to combat the existential despair that descends when we realize we alone aren't going to be able to solve problems like world hunger, genocide, or educational neglect. By reminding ourselves that behind every number and statistic is a profusion of unique individuals, each every bit as valuable as Zlata Filipović or Anne Frank, we are best able to recognize the concrete need for intervention and to think clearly about what we can do to ease the plight of someone in trouble. As a result, we are primed to take heroic or altruistic action.

Paul Slovic is fond of telling two stories that illustrate the human capacity for selfless intervention. In the first, a man fell into an icy lake; another driver saw him and jumped into the freezing water to save him. In the second, an elk fell through the ice, and several people stopped to pull it out. He's thought a lot about what motivated the rescuers to do what they did. "They were acting heroically because [what happened] was in their immediate vicinity," he says. "People are motivated to do heroic things when they *can* do them." A face, a concrete story or connection, a chat over coffee: All of these things can help us move from a state of emotional numbness, where action feels impossible, to a state of psychological closeness and personal investment, where generous and heroic measures feel not only more possible, but much more necessary. Inspired by contemplative practices thousands of years old, a growing contingent of researchers is learning that one way to achieve that elusive sense of investment and connection may be—paradoxically—to turn inward.

Chapter Four
INNER FOCUS AND COMPASSIONATE ACTION

I n a classroom at Stanford University's Li Ka Shing Center, a couple dozen of us are fanned out around the teacher, Kelly McGonigal, in one giant half moon of chairs—students in one of the first compassion cultivation training classes Stanford has offered to the public. Last week, we spent the initial class session talking about why we want to become more compassionate. Our homework assignment for the past week has been to meditate, focusing on the in-and-out sensation of our breath for fifteen minutes every day. With work and life commitments, though, it's been easy to let that practice fall by the wayside. I dread having to admit to the class that I haven't meditated every day.

But McGonigal, a Stanford psychologist and yoga teacher, isn't interested in calling people out. Instead, she puts us into small groups to talk about how the homework went. Then she has us meditate by closing our eyes and breathing deeply for five minutes, ending with a *gong* sound from an electronic timer. "Now," McGonigal prompts, as we rouse ourselves from our brief reverie, "what do you think this kind of meditation has to do with developing compassion?"

I think about how focusing on the breath helps us stay connected to the present moment—which is exactly the kind of immediate awareness we need to have in order to show compassion. Trying to maintain extended focus helps us deal better with getting distracted, which is what happens in real-life situations that call for compassion: when children tug on our arms during a phone conversation with a friend, when we rush past a homeless woman on our way to work. So while dedicated compassion meditation practices exist to help us concentrate on the suffering of others, a simple breath-focused meditation can also help by enhancing our ability to train our focus outside ourselves.

"There's something about noticing your own resistance and deciding to stay put with it that relates to compassion," McGonigal says, breaking into my thoughts. "We're training that key quality of awareness that needs to be present in order for compassion to unfold." Focusing on a single entity like the breath, she adds, can give us a feeling of being connected to something larger than our individual lives. "We have this experience that everything that happens in the world is revolving around our heads. Practicing gives us access to a level of awareness that is not so bound up in that sense of self."

While the meditation-centric compassion cultivation course I'm attending is fresh out of experimental trials, thinkers all over the world have noted the relationship between meditation and compassion for thousands of years. The Buddhist practice called *tonglen*, which involves focusing on the suffering of others and mentally sending them peace and goodwill, has long been said to improve practitioners' capacity to show compassion in real life. Other religious traditions feature similar practices. Meditating regularly, the theory goes, deepens your inner reservoir of compassion and may also increase your capacity to perform selfless acts in everyday life—some large enough in scope that they may even qualify as truly heroic. Take the World

War II–era Dutch Jewish mystic Etty Hillesum, a meditator who went on to strengthen and encourage countless fellow prisoners in the Westerbork concentration camp. Once preoccupied with dozens of minor, self-focused worries and concerns, she broadened her capacity to care for others with the help of her contemplative practice, establishing herself as the "thinking heart" of Westerbork camp before she was deported to Auschwitz, where she later died. In her mission to minister to fellow camp inmates, she became a hero to many fellow Jews who experienced her caring and concern firsthand—and, later, a hero to many thousands of readers worldwide who read her posthumously published diaries and letters. "Sometimes I might sit down beside someone, put an arm round a shoulder, say very little and just look into their eyes. Nothing was alien to me, not one single expression of human sorrow," she wrote. "People said to me, 'You must have nerves of steel to stand up to it.' I don't think I have nerves of steel, far from it, but I can certainly 'stand up to things.' I am not afraid to look suffering straight in the eyes."

Until recently, individual practitioners' reports contained the most compelling evidence for the connection between meditation and compassion. But with the advent of fMRI scanners like the one I visited in Bill Harbaugh's lab, as well as other advanced technology, researchers are beginning to get a sense of how sustained periods of intense meditative focus actually affect the way we think. One pioneer in this new field of meditation science is Richard Davidson, the founder of the Center for Investigating Healthy Minds at the University of Wisconsin–Madison. The day I visit him—a bitter-cold February afternoon—he welcomes me into his office, which is brimful of late-winter light despite the outdoor chill. His gray hair rises up from his scalp in defiant waves, and a thin strand of deep-red cord circles one of his wrists, coordinating with a garland of brightly colored prayer-flags hanging behind his desk.

Davidson, who has himself practiced meditation for more than thirty years, became intrigued by the practice's power to change mental outlook when he visited India as a graduate student. While on spiritual retreat there, he meditated for hours each day and came back feeling restored in a way he'd never dreamed possible. He decided he wanted to do an in-depth scientific study of meditation and its effects.

But when Davidson floated the idea, he got shot down. *Too woo-woo* was the gist of the feedback. "The zeitgeist was not right," he says, chuckling. "It was made very clear to me that if I wanted a successful career in science, this was not a good way to begin."

Davidson set the idea aside and turned to more general study of the neural roots of emotion, but his old dream rekindled after he first met the Dalai Lama in 1992. The Buddhist leader heard about Davidson's early studies of the neural basis of emotion and wondered if he could push his work in a new direction. "He said, 'Look, you're using the tools of neuroscience to investigate anxiety and fear; why can't you use them to investigate kindness and compassion?'" Davidson remembers.

Davidson gradually began laying the necessary groundwork to meet the Dalai Lama's challenge. In 2008, he founded the Center for Investigating Healthy Minds, an organization devoted to studying the origins of kindness, compassion, forgiveness, and mindfulness and exploring how to cultivate them. Before that, though, he conducted experiments focused on whether compassion meditation can change the way the brain functions. Anecdotal evidence abounded—long-term compassion meditators reported being more concerned with other people's suffering and more likely to help those in need—but Davidson wanted to explore the matter more scientifically.

To begin with, he invited a French Buddhist monk named Matthieu Ricard to his lab and had his assistant attach more than a hundred electrodes to Ricard's head. When the assistant asked Ricard to meditate on compassion and loving-kindness, his brain began to respond in a very unusual way: It produced strong gamma waves, a type of brain signal that reveals focused thinking. Other monks' brains showed a similar response.

Encouraged by these results, Davidson decided to probe more deeply into what the brain was doing during compassion meditation. He assembled a group of sixteen people who had spent years learning compassion-meditation techniques; all had amassed at least ten thousand hours of meditation over their lifetimes. He also recruited sixteen control subjects who had no meditation experience and were taught the basics of compassion meditation shortly before the experiment.

All of the participants, long- and short-term meditators alike, were instructed to get into the fMRI scanner at the University of Wisconsin and start practicing (or not practicing) compassion meditation. As they lay in the scanner, Davidson and his colleagues piped in an array of sounds. Some were neutral—background chatter in a restaurant—but others were chosen specifically to elicit empathy, such as the cry of a woman in distress. The scanner recorded activity in different areas of the participants' brains as they meditated and listened to the sounds.

Davidson found that when the long-term meditators were meditating and listening to sounds designed to provoke an emotional reaction, their brains showed large amounts of activity in the insula, a brain region that's involved in experiencing emotion, and also in the temporal parietal junction, an area that may be involved in empathy and understanding others' emotional states. The short-term meditators, on the other hand—even though they were familiar with the basic principles of compassion meditation—did not show such strong activation when listening to the emotionally charged sounds.

Davidson thinks his results support the theory that consistent compassion meditation training may make it easier to understand what other people are going through—and potentially motivate us to intervene when someone else is in distress. It's intriguing, he says, that compassion meditators with a higher level of expertise may be more attuned to suffering in those around them. "We don't know whether the systematic practice results in structural changes in the brain, but there's no question that there are differences in patterns of activation."

But Davidson's findings have not met with universal acclaim. Yi Rao, formerly a neuroscientist at Northwestern University, has called Davidson's work "substandard" in the press and criticized him for being a "politically involved scientist." At the time, Davidson—who says he does not consider himself a Buddhist—countered that Chinese opposition to the Dalai Lama was motivating some people to speak out against the Buddhist leader's involvement in neuroscience.

Controversy surrounding the Dalai Lama and Davidson's own motivations will likely continue to simmer, but Davidson is more focused on generating a torrent of new data than on quieting critics. With the help of a new $1.7 million grant from the John Templeton Foundation, he plans to study, among other things, whether a compassion meditation course makes a measurable impact on practitioners' everyday lives—on whether they make more altruistic choices in decision-making tasks than nonmeditators, for example. He acknowledges that it's difficult to study meditation's real-life effects without cloistering participants in a lab, but he's come up with some ingenious ways to test the practice's impact in the real world. He and his team are considering sending text messages to study participants, for instance, asking them to describe what they're feeling or doing at the exact moment they receive the text. The scientists will also record subjects' voices at random times throughout the day, which should provide insight into their emotional state (participants won't know precisely when their voices are being sampled).

More than a thousand people will participate in the sweeping studies CIHM has planned, designed as a pioneering large-scale analysis of whether laboratory measurements of brain changes translate into real differences in how subjects engage with the world. While Davidson hesitates to make specific predictions about whether meditation will engender greater day-to-day compassion in experiments, it's clear he has an idea. He's already advocating for new school curricula that will feature meditation-based components. "There's more and more evidence that cultivating social and emotional skills is more important for life success than cultivating cognitive skills." Practices such as compassion meditation, he believes, affect the way people relate to one another profoundly enough to warrant a social revolution. "The best possible outcome," he says, "would be the kindling of interest in this area in a way which would promote the integration of these practices in the mainstream of major institutions in our culture."

In Kelly McGonigal's Stanford class, we're starting to progress from simple breath-focused contemplation to specifically compassion-oriented meditation. During the third session, McGonigal announces that we're going to learn to meditate on feeling compassion for a loved one. To introduce us to this practice, McGonigal asks us to close our eyes and picture the suffering of someone we care about.

All of the exercises we've done up to this point have induced a sense of calm in me, but I'm surprised at how agitated I get during this short meditation. I think of a relative who's had a very difficult year— her father, who suffers from advanced dementia, has spent the last few months in hospital wards and nursing homes. As I think about the agony she must have been in, trying to make the best care decisions for her dad, I can feel tears welling in my eyes. It hits me once again: the impossibility of the dilemmas she's been confronted with, the loss of someone she has loved for so long.

When the meditation is over, I look around, blinking, and realize some of my classmates are also tearing up. McGonigal asks the class what it was like to face the reality of someone else's suffering head-on.

"Powerlessness," someone says.

"A sense I want to stop it."

"You try to temper it, hold it at bay a little bit."

"It can feel overwhelming, to the point where you want to back off."

McGonigal reassures us all this is normal—and, in fact, that learning to subsist in the presence of other people's suffering instead of instinctively trying to push it away is a key part of developing compassion. "When most people are made aware of suffering, the first thing we look for is escape. So we're going to start to cultivate a specific set of responses to suffering that will allow us to stay put." The ability to stay put during suffering, I reflect, seems like an important asset for would-be heroes and altruists. Without the ability to remain present, to process the full extent of an injustice that's taking place, how can we possibly motivate ourselves to take action to right that injustice or ease that person's pain?

Later, McGonigal's co-teacher, the Stanford researcher Leah Weiss Ekstrom, adds another step to this basic meditation. First she asks us to pick a loved one and picture them suffering, as we did before. Then she instructs us to picture ourselves sending peace and happiness to this person. She tells us to repeat a sequence of phrases inside our heads: "May you be happy. May you be at peace. May you be free from suffering." As we concentrate on sending these feelings out, she has us focus on the gentle expansion and contraction of our chests. We pretend we're breathing in and breathing out directly through them, as if there's an opening in our hearts through which the compassionate wishes can flow.

I do feel a little more magnanimous when I try this practice, but

I'm still concerned that I'm not feeling as compassionate as I should. When I chant, "May you be happy. May you be at peace. May you be free from suffering" to myself, the rote words seem to get in the way, preventing the natural rush of tenderness I feel when I'm in the presence of a real person. It's hard to summon up those feelings from scratch, just like it's hard to summon on-the-spot compassion for the homeless people I walk past on the street.

At least a few of my classmates seem to feel the same way. "I can't evoke the feelings like I can if I'm *with* my daughter," someone says. It's almost as if the very act of trying to conjure up the emotion prevents it from appearing, much as sitting at your desk trying to get work done makes you want to do just about anything else. Also, visualizing sending out waves of compassion feels uncomfortably New Agey and stilted. "It feels a little hokey, like I'm shooting beams of light at my friend," one guy confesses.

"With some of us, the aspirational phrases may not sit right," Ekstrom says. McGonigal tells us to ditch the phrases if we need to and simply call up whatever words, images, and memories allow us to generate caring for the person we're thinking about. She assures us that we can summon this sense of caring without feeling as if our heartstrings are being tugged on every second. "Some people will be nonemotional, and some people will be flooding with joy and emotion. You don't have to feel anything, and the practice is still doing something."

While the results of Davidson's large-scale meditation studies will not appear for several years, researchers are already finding preliminary indications that meditating may lead to measurable changes in the way we lead our lives—especially in how likely we are to reach out to others in need. When the Stanford psychologist Jeanne Tsai, the graduate student Birgit Koopmann-Holm, and their colleagues gave meditators and nonmeditators the opportunity to write to a convicted murderer who'd admitted his guilt in a letter, 67 percent of the meditators took advantage of the chance to write, whereas only 44 percent of the nonmeditators did. The meditators weren't just more likely to write; they also wrote longer letters that displayed more empathy and forgiveness toward the murderer.

To investigate the meditation-compassion connection further, the researchers performed a second study in which subjects were assigned to one of four groups. The first group took a compassion meditation class two hours a week for eight weeks, the second group took a mindfulness meditation class for the same length of time, the third group took an improvisational theater class, and the fourth took no class at all. Afterward the team analyzed the letters subjects wrote to the convicted murderer and found that members of the compassion meditation group were more encouraging toward him than members of the three other groups. The statements the meditators made expressed hope that the murderer would be able to rise above his self-created circumstances and salvage a meaningful life.

Meanwhile, Tsai's Stanford colleagues—the researchers Hooria Jazaieri, Philippe Goldin, and others—have specifically assessed the effectiveness of the type of CCT class I've been taking, and the early analysis is intriguing. In before-and-after assessments, they evaluated people's self-reported tendencies in three areas: fear of showing compassion for others, fear of showing compassion to themselves, and fear of accepting compassion from others. Students showed improvement on all three of these scales after taking the course, indicating that they were more receptive overall to the idea of showing compassion. Anecdotally, too, participants testified that CCT helped awaken their feelings of affinity for others and dampen feelings of discord. "I was able to turn loose a lot of my hatred I have for a neighbor. I found myself contemplating ways of killing him," one military veteran who took the course said afterward. "I have now lost all that hatred. It's only hurting me, not him." And following a similar compassion meditation course at Emory University, participants showed an enhanced ability to correctly interpret the meaning of other people's facial expressions, a kind of empathic accuracy that may help foster strong social relationships. Compassion meditators in an Emory study who had higher-than-average practice times also had lower levels of the stress-related compound interleukin-6 in their blood after stress exposure, which suggests that dedicated meditation practice may help relax high-alert responses.

But on the central question—are people who take courses like this more inclined to take compassionate *action* in the real world, to intervene regularly when someone needs help?—the jury is still out. One sticking point is that the scientific vocabulary needed to make such a determination is still being refined. Emiliana Simon-Thomas, a researcher at UC Berkeley's Greater Good Science Center, points out that the research community has had a tough time creating a consensus scale to measure compassion. Simply asking someone how compassionate they feel after taking a CCT course, Simon-Thomas says, isn't likely to elicit an accurate response—many people claim they're more compassionate than they actually are in order to make themselves look good. "With the self-report data, you're pretty limited," Simon-Thomas says. There's social desirability around representing yourself as compassionate."

Researchers are trying a number of tactics to get around this problem. One is a video game developed by Tania Singer of Germany's Max Planck Institute and others, which assesses people's level of "prosociality" by recording game-time decisions about whether the character they control is willing to help another character. Another is an assessment of people's implicit attitudes. Instead of asking subjects straight out, "Do you think it's more important to pursue your own self-interest or the well-being of the community?" Simon-Thomas might, for example, show people the word "caring" and ask them to judge as quickly as possible whether that word fits into the category of "me" or "not me." People's split-second reactions in scenarios like these can reveal quite a bit about their unspoken, unconscious attitudes, so the approach may someday offer a predictive glimpse at whether test-takers are more apt post-CCT to extend themselves for someone else's benefit. There's intriguing new evidence that they may actually do so. In a *Psychological Science* study, people who took a compassion meditation course were more likely to give money to others in need in an experimental online game.

Studies of whether course graduates actually *do* behave more compassionately in their everyday lives would take months to years and involve intensive follow-up, but CCT planners are determined to forge ahead in the interim, fueled by their deep-rooted conviction that compassion training has the potential to make a true impact. Their contention is a bold and potentially transformative one: CCT wakes us up to the suffering of our fellow humans, softening our hearts and supplying us with the motivation we need to relieve that suffering. "This meets huge needs. It isn't fringe anymore—people are ready for it," Ekstrom says. "A real paradigm shift could happen."

The compassion cultivation training class is drawing to a close—it's our eighth session. After progressing through breath-focused meditation and meditation on other people's suffering, we're finally ready to be introduced to the full-blown practice of compassion meditation, or *tonglen*, as Buddhist followers and others around the world practice it.

The practice, as McGonigal explains it, is simple. When you witness someone suffering or in pain, you take a deep breath and imagine yourself taking in the person's anguish. Then, as you breathe out, you imagine sending out peace and happiness. You can confine *tonglen* to a single individual, or you can broaden your focus, sending peace and fulfillment to all members of suffering groups: single mothers struggling to make ends meet, refugees trying to patch their war-torn lives back together, people who have failed to achieve the goals they've dreamed of. Finally, when you feel ready, you can expand your compassionate focus to include the entire population of the planet.

To help us get a feel for *tonglen*, McGonigal has us pick some example of suffering we're experiencing in our own lives, then concentrate on inhaling that suffering and breathing out compassion for ourselves. It feels strange to purposely open my heart to suffering—I'm still so used to pushing suffering away when it appears, to drowning it out with distractions or rationalizations, that I can tell completely letting it in will take more practice.

"How did it feel to breathe in suffering?" McGonigal asks.

We look around at one another. "My mind would ricochet off," one woman says. "I'd have to bring it back. I didn't want to stay there."

McGonigal assures the questioner her resistance is normal. "A willingness to be with your own difficult experiences is the foundation for having compassion for others."

One man reports that the practice allowed him to feel more connected with others. "Not only am I not alone, but I'm also able to help someone else. You know that you're better suited to potentially understand someone's pain."

We move on to doing the practice with a partner from the class. I end up being paired with a man I'll call Craig, whom I've spoken to in passing a couple of times, but don't know very well. This time, instead of asking us to think of our own suffering, McGonigal asks us to think about the suffering the person sitting across from us has experienced. I close my eyes and conjure up an image of Craig, his chest rising and falling with the flow of his breath.

It strikes me that he has probably gotten through many difficult times in his life, just as I have. That suffering is pretty much unavoidable, regardless of our parentage or our family's means, our appearance or our intelligence. I mouth the phrases to myself, directing them to Craig in my mind—*may you be happy, may you be at peace, may you be free from suffering*—and this time, they seem imbued with meaning, not the rote words they were at the outset.

The more I can relate someone else's suffering to something difficult I've been through, the easier it is for me to feel compassion for that person. Maybe that's part of what *tonglen* does. It encourages us to breathe in the suffering of others in order to remind us what that suffering must have been like, much as a whiff of sea breeze can conjure up an entire oceanside landscape in our minds. Over time, what seems to happen is that we get comfortable enough with the idea of that suffering to remain in its presence in real life. In one of my favorite books, Chaim Potok's *The Chosen*, the main character Danny's rabbi father raises him in near-silence so he can learn to hear the suffering of the world. It seems like this is what *tonglen*, too, is all about: learning to hear the suffering of the world, allowing it to pry open your heart and make it more responsive to others' plights.

Just as Paul Slovic might have predicted, I find it easier to empathize with the suffering of individuals than large groups of people during *tonglen*, especially with people I know who have recently been through a difficult time. As soon as I try to broaden my focus—to send peace and fulfillment to all cancer sufferers, all infertile women, all widows—an aperture in my mind seems to close just a little. It's as if my brain can't handle that degree of suffering, so it decides not to let it in. Or maybe it's just harder for me to picture faceless, identityless members of a group suffering than it is to picture real people.

As I progress with my meditation practice, I surprise myself by doing things I'm pretty sure I wouldn't do had I not been meditating.

I'm a volunteer mentor to high school students, and last year, one of my mentees was missing in action most of the time, almost never responding to my phone calls. I assumed she just didn't want to spend time with me, and I felt like a bad mentor. I'd never tried to get in touch with her after the program ended.

About twenty minutes after one of my meditation sessions, I leave a simple comment on a photo she posted on Facebook: "You look lovely and happy. Hope you are doing well." She responds almost instantly, and to my surprise, we end up having a long conversation and setting a time to get together for dinner—something I'd never have dreamed was possible before I took the compassion training class.

I'm not sure yet whether I will manage to keep up my compassion meditation practice, but I'm motivated to stick with it because it helps me look at the world differently, cutting through the relentless self-focus that has dogged me most of my life and gently retraining my focus where I want it to be—on other people. "There is a sense that when you breathe in suffering, it is transformed just by the connection to something bigger than you," McGonigal tells us. Our own suffering is like a rock, she says. "When we breathe in the suffering of others, it's like that rock is dissolving into smaller pieces and it just flows through." I assumed that learning to bear the suffering of those around me would be a key prerequisite for taking compassionate action, but what I never expected is the way developing an increased tolerance for other people's pain makes my *own* pain seem less dire, less shattering. It's a perspective shift I want to maintain, regardless of whether I ever manage to join the ranks of the heroic and altruistic elite.

My new experience with compassion meditation gets me thinking more about the connections between suffering and becoming a better person. Opening ourselves up to our own pain and that of others, the CCT curriculum teaches, is critical in motivating ourselves to relieve that pain. I'm still curious, though, about whether there's real evidence that suffering transforms us, awakens our selfless impulses by allowing us to understand others' pain more fully. Examining that question introduces me to an under-the-radar collective of sufferers—scientists and nonscientists alike—who've turned the painful dross of their lives into heroic and altruistic gold.

Chapter Five
SUFFERING AND HEROISM

For some people, school memories prompt a wave of rose-tinted nostalgia, but what Jodee Blanco remembers clearly is willing herself to make it to the end of each day. Every lunch period, she'd sit on the sink in the girls' bathroom and wolf down a candy bar, knowing no one would let her sit at their cafeteria table. Members of the football and wrestling teams would pin her on the ground and cram handfuls of snow into her mouth. One school heartthrob signed her yearbook, "You'll have to fuck yourself, we hate you, bitch." When she rebuked a teacher for poking fun at a special-ed student, he laughed at her and retorted, "No wonder you're such a loser." "Most people assume that the hardest part is the abuse you take," Blanco says now, decades later. "The hardest part was all the friendship I had to give that nobody wanted. It backed up in my system like a toxin."

As an adult, Blanco worked hard to leave her horrendous school experience behind. She built her own public relations and consulting company, The Blanco Group, and became a publicist for *New York Times* bestsellers. Garnering the attention of important people and major publishing houses, she finally had the social acceptance she'd always wanted.

But after she saw footage of the shootings at Colorado's Columbine High School in 1999, Blanco found herself delving once again into her difficult past. Angry that the media seemed to be missing the role bullying played in turning kids like Eric Harris and Dylan Klebold into school shooters, she decided to write a book that chronicled the horrific impact of bullying on her own life. She hoped the book would alert parents and educators to the magnitude of the problem—and that it might help save other kids from the hell she'd gone through.

The book Blanco wrote, *Please Stop Laughing at Me*, hit shelves in 2003, and from the start, its appeal defied her modest predictions. Within two days of its release, it landed on the *New York Times* best-seller list, thanks in part to a word-of-mouth campaign among students, parents, and teachers. The massive groundswell of interest convinced Blanco her book was truly a reflection of a wider social problem that wasn't being sufficiently addressed. "I received hundreds of e-mails from people all over the U.S. who were being bullied," she says. When one young correspondent, a sixth-grade girl from Minnesota, confided to Blanco that she was suicidal, Blanco swung into action. She contacted administrators at the girl's school and told them what was going on. "The principal said, 'Oh my God, tell me what to do.' I said, 'Let me come to the school and surprise this child.'"

Not only did Blanco make a trip to the girl's school to meet her in person, she also gave a presentation to other students there about the impact bullying had had on her life and the importance of treating others with respect. Other schools started calling to have her come speak, and these first few appearances eventually evolved into a more formal anti-bullying program called "It's NOT Just Joking Around!" To date, more than half a million students, teachers, and parents have seen her share her story in school gymnasiums and auditoriums across the country. In a typical ninety-minute school presentation, Blanco acts out painful episodes from her past—a strategy, she says, that helps bullies understand they're damaging victims for life and assures victims that if she survived, so can they. "Imagine how you're hurting the feelings of your classmates who you laugh at every day and don't even realize that you're snickering or laughing at them, because it's so second nature," she tells one audience of high school students, pacing back and forth across the auditorium floor. "It is not just joking around. You are damaging each other." Her forehead crinkles as she recounts how a fellow classmate told her she was "God's worst mistake," and her eyes fill with tears. Following her presentation and questions from the audience, she often does one-on-one interventions with a variety of kids—perpetrators, bystanders, and victims—who've found themselves in the middle of various bullying scenarios.

Blanco relishes the life she currently leads, writing, speaking, and traveling around the country to champion effective anti-bullying strategies. The irony, she reflects now, is that had it not been for her miserable school experience, she never would have made helping bullied students her life's work. When she thinks about her past, she feels gratitude instead of anger. "My goal is to turn my pain into purpose," she says. "I can look at my life and say, 'Wow, I was meant to be bullied. Look at what it did. I'm able to save lives.' Instead of resenting your past, you accept it as a fundamental part of your destiny."

To the kids who read her books and hear her speak, Jodee Blanco is a hero. She receives thousands of letters from students all over the country and the world, thanking her for speaking out on their behalf and helping them realize they are not alone. Under the right circumstances, philosophers and mystics have long argued, pain and suffering can serve as catalysts that awaken generous and heroic impulses within us. "When we feel wretched, that softens us up," the Buddhist monk and spiritual teacher Pema Chodron writes. "It ripens our hearts. It becomes the ground for understanding others."

This perspective is often drowned out by the scores of different cultural voices that insist we should strive to excise psychological pain from our lives much as we might extract a rotting tooth. An entire industry—buoyed by self-help books, therapists, and health spas—has sprung up with the direct or implied purpose of eliminating stress and suffering.

But looking deeper, delving into age-old stories that run like thrumming wires through the cultural landscape, we find ample acknowledgment of the strength and compassion suffering can awaken. In "hero's journey" narratives like *The Aeneid*, protagonists typically undergo a series of painful ordeals so they can gird themselves for the final battle, the one that tests their strength, courage, and selflessness to the utmost. And many fictional action heroes have a suffering-inspired past: Spider-Man's alter ego, Peter Parker, is a nerdy kid who deals with his share of rejection at school, while Bruce Wayne, who later becomes Batman, sees his parents killed when he is eight. Similarly, when the researcher Pilar Hernandez-Wolfe examined the lives of thirty-five Colombian human rights activists, she found that many of them had episodes of intense struggle in their personal histories—episodes that, in some cases, helped convince them to devote their lives to helping others.

When we suffer and eventually heal, we undergo profound psychological changes. The depths of our own pain, while often excruciating, make it easier for us to understand exactly what other people are feeling when they're in danger or despair. As a result, we can become more empathetic people, better able to assist others when they encounter their own seemingly impassable obstacles. This kind of hard-won experience, Blanco says, is exactly what has made her an effective anti-bullying advocate. "Let's say you were walking down the street, you fell into a hole, and two people offered to help," she says. "One was a renowned academic who had written a paper on the dynamics of holes, and the other was an average person who had fallen into the same hole and was offering to climb back down, grab your hand, and guide you out the same way *he* found. Whose help would you want?"

Miep Gies, who helped Anne Frank's family hide from the Nazis, also pointed to difficult circumstances that were instrumental in her decision to become a rescuer. When she was a girl, she lived through severe post–World War I food shortages in Austria, and her parents decided to send her to the Netherlands, where there was more to eat. "I still remember the hunger pangs distinctly, the piercing pains in my stomach and the unpleasant fits of dizziness I had to try to overcome," Gies wrote. She recalled the wrenching pain of being sent from Austria to Holland to live with a family who could feed her. "My parents . . . hung a big sign with a strange name on it around my neck, said goodbye, and left me. They had no other choice, of course, but I did not understand that until much later."

While I've never undergone terrible hardship or privation, my interest in a possible connection between suffering and altruism arose after I slogged through a bout of depression several years ago. I barely ate for about two months and spent entire days lying on the couch. During the worst of the depression, it never occurred to me that anything good could come of it; I was mostly focused on keeping myself going from day to day. But as I began to emerge from this dark period, I realized that I now had a much better idea of what other depressed people were going through, having experienced some of it myself— and I was able to put that knowledge into practice much sooner than I expected. When I had a high school mentee who was dealing with depression and anxiety attacks, I was able to empathize and reassure her much more convincingly than I ever could have before. Eventually,

I was able to feel grateful for the way my depression had shaped me, helped clue me in to the suffering of others, even if it had felt like hell at the time.

While it might seem counterintuitive that suffering breeds self-lessness and, in some noteworthy cases, heroism, science is beginning to support this notion. People who have undergone significant suffering may emerge from the experience with higher levels of empathy, a more positive orientation toward others, and a conviction that they are personally responsible for others' welfare. In his surveys, Zimbardo has found that survivors of a disaster or a personal trauma are three times more likely to be heroes and volunteers.

No researcher has delved more deeply into the connection between suffering and subsequent selflessness than Ervin Staub, a former University of Massachusetts Amherst professor of psychology who received his Ph.D. at Stanford. "We were very scientific," he says in a gentle European accent. "I didn't even dare to think about the personal roots. But everything I've done arises from personal roots."

Those roots extend back to 1944, when Staub was six years old and living in Budapest, Hungary, with his Jewish family. Jews had been targeted by an increasingly restrictive series of laws: they had to wear a yellow star badge, they were not allowed to ride public transportation, and they could not even listen to the radio. One evening, thugs raced to capture his thirteen-year-old cousin when she was caught trying to buy bread after the Jewish curfew; she escaped only by ducking into her family's home. By the summer of 1944, Jews from all over Hungary were being deported to the death camp at Auschwitz, and the fate of Budapest's Jews hung in the balance.

It was during this turbulent year that Staub benefited from an act of heroism that has since become world-famous. Raoul Wallenberg, a secretary at Budapest's Swedish legation, decided to take action after learning that Nazi officials intended to deport about 200,000 Jews from the city. Knowing that Nazi authorities tended to respect seemingly official symbols, he designed a Swedish "protective pass" for Jews. Any bearer of this pass was to be considered under the protection of the Swedish government and therefore exempt from deportation.

Wallenberg issued thousands of his protective passes to Budapest's Jews, and Staub and his family managed to secure some, shielding them from deportation orders that almost certainly would have meant death. Near the end of the war, Budapest's Jews were sent on a death march toward the heart of the Third Reich, but the Staubs escaped this fate, moving into a "protected house" Wallenberg had set up. There they were sustained by a Christian woman named Maria, who stayed with them and risked her own life to make sure they were fed, slipping them bread she'd cooked at a bakery on the sly. Her kindness affected young Ervin deeply, and he kept returning to a seemingly unanswerable question: Why would someone put her life on the line to save him and his family?

Staub eventually immigrated to the United States after the war, and his curiosity about the origins of altruism helped lead him to a career in psychology. For many years, he studied the topic of what leads people to help others, testing the importance of factors like environment and family influence. But his specific interest in what he calls "altruism born of suffering" was kindled around 1989, when *Psychology Today* magazine commissioned him to develop a questionnaire about helping behaviors. Thousands of readers sent back the finished questionnaire, and many also wrote letters to help explain their responses to the survey. One common theme struck Staub as he read through the letters. "People were saying, 'I want to help others because I suffered, and I don't want other people to suffer the way I have suffered.'"

Was it possible, Staub wondered, that people could actually become *more* altruistic, more willing to help others, as a result of having undergone a difficult experience themselves? It initially seemed like an uncertain proposition. Some previous research suggested that people who had been harmed tended to become aggressive and violent. And hard-won experience had taught him that not everyone who suffered became more sensitive to others' needs—far from it. It was very easy to shut down and turn bitter when you were in pain, to focus exclusively on your own survival.

Yet there is also compelling evidence that, in some cases, suffering might awaken heightened concern for others. When the social scientist Zora Raboteg-Šarić and her colleagues studied five- and six-year-old Croatian children in the wake of the warfare there in the early 1990s, they displayed more prosocial behavior after the war's outbreak than they had before it. And when the Indiana University of Pennsylvania psychologist Krys Kaniasty studied one thousand Hurricane Hugo victims and nonvictims, victims reported engaging in more helping. The victims also provided high levels of tangible and emotional support to others.

Curious about whether his "altruism born of suffering" theory held water, Staub designed his own study. He and his colleague Johanna Vollhardt asked subjects whether they'd ever been victims of natural disasters or experienced violence. They also asked the respondents whether they felt empathy for victims of the recent Southeast Asian tsunami and whether they felt a responsibility to help these victims. It turned out that respondents who'd experienced trauma themselves—whether as a result of natural disaster or violence—were significantly more likely to express empathy for the tsunami victims. They were also more likely to put their empathy into action by signing up to collect money for tsunami survivors.

Why do some people who have endured great suffering make the heroic effort to go out of their way to help people they don't know?

What compels them to make this leap? One important precondition, Staub says, is that sufferers need to heal from their wounds and regain their trust in others—at least to a certain extent—before they can turn the raw material of suffering into heightened empathy. Some resilient individuals, for instance, nurture strong relationships with parents, spouses, or other important people in their lives. Others may reach out for help through support groups or other social networks and build trusting ties that way. Once basic psychological needs are fulfilled, including the need for food, security, and close human contact, people tend to be more capable of focusing on the needs of those outside their immediate sphere.

People's experiences during or immediately after a painful event may also determine whether or not they later rise to the occasion and transform their suffering into compassion. When people receive help from others in a difficult time, for instance, it may renew their faith in humanity to such an extent that they feel compelled to bring the same relief to others. Being helped provides people with helper role models whom they emulate later on—it was no accident, for example, that Miep Gies helped the Franks after a Dutch family nursed her back from starvation as a child. "If other people help you at the time you are victimized, that tells you the world is not all like the people that are harming you, that there is caring," Staub says. Close, loving relationships *prior* to a difficult event, such as strong family ties, may also increase the odds that sufferers will turn their pain into goodwill. "They have this template, so to speak, about the possibility of experiencing love and caring. Those experiences in early childhood can create a certain degree of resilience."

Perhaps just as important is how we process the bad things that happen to us and whether we consciously decide to create redeeming meaning from them. To tip the balance toward openhearted altruism rather than defensiveness and emotional shutdown, we need to face pain head-on rather than denying it or turning to coping mechanisms like drugs and alcohol to blot it out. Writing about painful experiences or talking about them with supportive friends helps us distinguish the past from the present, allowing us to come to terms with what has happened and move on. Acknowledging our own pain is an essential step that motivates us to alleviate similar pain in others.

People who wonder about how to transform their own suffering into altruism or heroism, Staub believes, tend to be the ones who have what it takes to do so: an ability to step outside traumatic experience—either while it is happening, or after some time has passed—and contemplate what it has shown them about what's most important in life and what their *own* mission should be. The psychiatrist Viktor Frankl, who was deported from Czechoslovakia to the Auschwitz concentration camp in 1944, is perhaps the best-known pioneer of this approach. In the midst of misery, death, and starvation at the camp, Frankl concluded that life was still meaningful, and he turned his extreme suffering into a catalyst for renewed love and appreciation of others. "Suffering ceases to be suffering at the moment it finds a meaning," he wrote in a reflective chronicle of his experiences, *Man's Search for Meaning*, that later became a worldwide bestseller. "Frankl said to himself, 'I'm going to take notes about this because I want to use this to make a difference in the world,'" Staub says. "But that requires someone who's oriented in a certain way, who's not overwhelmed by their experience." One way to put difficult experiences into context, to avoid being swept into their undertow, is to view them from a universal perspective: For every setback we undergo—a job loss, an assault, an abandonment—thousands or millions of human beings all over the world have almost certainly absorbed a blow just like it. Not only does this mind-set prevent us from feeling alone in our suffering, it increases our empathy for others in the same situation.

Staub has had his students write a variety of autobiographical papers over the years, which can evolve into vivid illustrations of how certain ways of gaining perspective on painful experiences can give rise to greater compassion and willingness to help others. One student, for example, wrote about being targeted in eighth grade by members of a clique of boys who would tease her and try to touch her as she walked by. The teachers were no help, shrugging: "Boys will be boys." At home, though, her parents expressed sympathy for what was happening and supported her through the whole ordeal. They also encouraged her to consider others' points of view; she came to realize that the boy leading the teasing and abuse received very little attention from his status-conscious parents at home.

The student believed that her past experiences, combined with the support she received throughout, made her more alert to both the prevalence of suffering and the potential to alleviate it—realizations that led her to undertake many different helping missions throughout her life. She's one of the first people others turn to for solace in times of trouble. She's also volunteered with a wide variety of charitable organizations and worked with troubled girls and mentally and physically disabled kids.

Staub's research on the suffering-altruism link has focused on victims: people who have been ostracized or attacked, or whose homes and families have been ravaged by natural disaster. But he thinks other common varieties of suffering, such as depression, job loss, or a family member's death, may also inspire us to reach out to others later on. "One of the consequences will be better awareness of others' suffering," he says. "And if you are helped in the course of your suffering, that generates a positive [orientation] toward others."

This kind of positive other-orientation is evident in poverty-stricken communities throughout the United States, where people who've suffered in a specific sense—experiencing financial hardship—are more apt to help others than their richer counterparts. The Berkeley psychologists Paul Piff, Dacher Keltner, and their colleagues found that members of the economic lower class are more likely to act altruistically than those with larger bank accounts and that poorer people also tend to score higher in measures of generosity and trust. Some charitable giving data supports this finding: Rich people give away a lower percentage of their income than poorer people do.

Why might people hovering near the poverty line be more likely to help their fellow humans? Part of it, Keltner thinks, is that poor people must often band together to make it through tough times—a process that probably makes them more socially astute. "When you face uncertainty, it makes you orient to other people," he says. "You build up these strong social networks." When a poor young mother has a new baby, for instance, she may need help securing food, supplies, and child care, and if she has healthy social ties, members of her community will pitch in. (Perhaps not coincidentally, poorer people are also better at assessing the emotions others convey through their facial expressions, which may make them more adept at understanding what others need.) But limited income is hardly a prerequisite for developing this kind of empathy and social responsiveness. Regardless of the size of our bank accounts, suffering becomes a conduit to altruism or heroism when our own pain compels us to be more attentive to other people's needs and to intervene when we see someone in the clutches of the kind of suffering we know so well.

In fact, the more intimately familiar we become with our suffering, the greater responsibility we can start to feel for other people in similar situations, as the remarkable trajectory of Jodee Blanco's life illustrates. Over the years, as she took stock of the horrible things that happened to her in school, she came to see her past suffering less as a source of painful memories and more as an invaluable qualification for helping others. All the stomach-churning flashbacks she endures as she acts out scenes from her adolescence are worth it, she believes, if she can drive her point home—if she can convince kids, even if only a handful in every audience, that the ripple effects of bullying extend farther than they ever could have imagined. Like Zeus and Demeter's daughter, Persephone, who was whisked off to the underworld when she least expected it and returned a changed person, Blanco has emerged from her time in hell more dedicated to her heroic quest in spite of—and in some ways *because* of—her brush with the worst life has to offer.

While suffering can be a reliable conduit to selflessness, these helping behaviors, in turn, have potential to supply us with the kind of deep life satisfaction Jodee Blanco's anti-bullying activism has given her. "If you use your pain to help others," she says, "instead of resenting your past, it makes you appreciate it in a whole different way." Dedicating your life to something larger than yourself, research shows, imparts a lasting sense of happiness and well-being—one that can sometimes be powerful enough to ward off depression, banish fatigue, and even add years to your life.

Chapter Six
HELPING, HEALTH, AND HAPPINESS

A few years ago, thirty-two-year-old Mike Hrostoski found himself hitting a major lull. Out of nowhere, his mom had died in her sleep at age fifty-seven, leaving him reeling and wondering if there was a point to it all. In spite of his grief, though, he wanted to make sure his younger brother, David, still had a great summer. The two of them decided to embark on a road trip where they would scatter their mom's ashes everywhere they went, see whatever they could, and enjoy spending time together.85

The trip was such a resounding success that Hrostoski found himself wanting to have more off-the-beaten-path adventures—so much so that in December 2011, he quit his corporate job. "It wasn't very satisfying. I was making great money, but spending a lot of time in the office." He wrote a blog post on his personal website, asking his readers, "What would you do if money wasn't an issue?"

Hrostoski was struck by how consistent the responses were. Most people said they'd want to do one of three things: volunteer, travel, or spend time with family. He liked the idea of serving others—it fit well with his resolution of spending the year in ways that made him feel alive and happy. So he and his brother began gearing up for a reprise summer road trip that would last three months, swing through thirty-five different cities, and take them over twelve thousand miles. They'd work as volunteers most days, offering their services to whichever local organizations and individuals were most in need. With help from social media contacts, Hrostoski set up a jam-packed itinerary that would take him and his brother to places like Habitat for Humanity construction sites, youth shelters, and nonprofit organizations. Instead of staying at hotels, the duo crashed with friends or couch-surfed.

Hrostoski had been looking forward to traveling again with his brother, but what he didn't anticipate was how great volunteering would make him feel or how much his outlook would change along the way. "When I was working my corporate job, only one or two hours a day would be feeling worthwhile," he says. "On this trip, every day was like twelve hours of stuff that makes me feel happy, makes me feel alive." A lot of that feeling, he thinks, came from the knowledge that he spent significant time to make other people's lives better. "There's the feeling of doing things that are good that makes me feel happy, and I'm learning so much about the world and about other people," he says. At a youth shelter in Des Moines, Iowa, for instance, some of the teenagers he got to know opened up to him about the tough times and abuse they'd endured. "It has been incredibly perspective-shifting. These are thirteen-year-old children and the stuff they've gone through, I've gone through nothing."

Despite the nonstop itinerary—he and his brother sometimes ended up volunteering about thirty hours a week, in addition to other activities—he said he felt better, mentally and physically, than he ever expected. "In terms of the schedule, it was grueling, but at the same time I was super-energized every day. I woke up, I felt great. I'd recommend it for anyone."

Talking with Hrostoski, I think back to the time six years ago when I first decided to get involved in the mentoring program for at-risk high school students in San Jose. Initially, I was apprehensive, learning I'd be matched up with two "at-risk youth" and would build a relationship with them over the course of a school year. What if my mentees and I didn't have anything in common? What if I was in way over my head?

My fears proved largely unfounded. What surprised me, though, was just how happy I felt because of my involvement in the program. I looked forward to "community meetings" when all the mentors and youth in the program would gather together, even though they sometimes involved waking up before 7:00 a.m. on a Saturday. Asking my mentees questions about school, taking them out to the art museum or a local coffee shop, advising them about how to tackle problems in their lives: All of it invigorated me, drowned out the typical background buzz of self-directed thoughts and worries. I found myself looking forward to their updates on their crazy little siblings, their tests and soccer matches, their ever-flowing stream of thoughts about the future.

Instead of focusing on what was wrong with my life, I focused on how I could improve someone else's—a mental shift that had a way of putting my other work and life concerns in perspective. At the end of one school year, one of the other volunteers, Tom, called to thank me for having been a part of the program. I was flattered, but felt in a way as if I didn't deserve the kudos. Volunteering—regardless of the good I was able to do—had essentially become a selfish act. "I feel like I get so much more out of the program than I give," I told Tom.

Hrostoski's experience and my own might surprise people who view community work as drudgery, but they don't shock Allan Luks in the slightest. For years, Luks and various social scientists have shown that people who devote themselves to helping others enjoy a high degree of life satisfaction. Volunteers, the data indicates, are healthier as well as happier than nonvolunteers, and a recent study suggests they may also live longer. When I broach the topic with Luks one rainy spring afternoon at Fordham's Manhattan campus, he nods knowingly; in nonprofit circles, he says, the finding that helping, health, and life satisfaction are intertwined is old news. "It's no different than nutrition, exercise. My job is not to tell you about new research. The research is there."

Using the data to convince people to take action is another matter entirely. Nonprofit organizations have long struggled to sign up and keep volunteers—the very community force that keeps them going. In Charlotte, North Carolina, the United Way reported a severe shortage of mentors for at-risk students in 2012, necessitating an all-out recruiting drive, and a volunteer ambulance service in central New York State was recently forced to shut down in part due to a lack of personnel. Perpetual recruiting shortfalls like these hint at a long-standing paradox of altruism: Science shows that it makes us happier, and individual participants agree, but the numbers deficits continue year after year. So where does the disparity between our feelings and our actions arise? Why don't we want to do the very thing that so dramatically improves the way we live?

Luks doesn't have a definitive answer to that question, but he's spent a lot of time pondering it. A Peace Corps veteran, a former community action lawyer, and onetime executive director of the national mentoring titan Big Brothers Big Sisters, he has as much firsthand experience with helping work as anyone. He currently helms the Fordham Center for Nonprofit Leaders, a continuing education program at the university's Graduate School of Social Service whose mission is to train business-savvy nonprofit heads. Still, for the first half hour we're together, I barely have a chance to bring up *his* ventures because he's so busy asking me questions about myself. How did I get the idea to write my book? Where am I living now? When he learns I'll be having a baby in the fall, we clink plastic glasses in the middle of Fordham's Lincoln Center cafeteria. I'm typing frantically to record his thoughts, but he insists I turn my attention to my wrap sandwich. "You need to finish that! Just let me talk while you eat."

Swallowing, I ask how he came to dedicate his life to public service. "What started me off was growing up during the civil rights era," he says. "I did some marches, I felt good about it." He'd worked in restaurants as a kid, socialized with many black employees, and realized quickly that they were just ordinary people like him. That made him sympathetic toward the burgeoning racial justice movement.

An outlet for those sympathetic impulses arose a few years later, when he and a few fellow Georgetown Law School students found themselves in rural North Carolina. Luks was researching an article for a school publication and wanted to learn if blacks in the area had the right to vote. He befriended a local black funeral-home owner who helped get him involved in overseeing voter registration procedures at the local courthouse. It was Luks's job to give out information about the registration process and reassure voters—even in the face of blatant intimidation from local members of the Ku Klux Klan. While playing an integral role in helping establish fairness, Luks was suffused with a sense of excitement and well-being.

After law school graduation, Luks headed to Venezuela with the Peace Corps and went on to become a community action lawyer in East Harlem, where he helped tenement dwellers organize to raise money for repairs that would supply their apartments with reliable heat and hot water. Grateful for his help and support, the building residents surprised him over the holidays with an expensive gift, moving him nearly to tears. "They gave me a Samsonite suitcase and said, "Here, you can put your legal papers in it.'"

In the late 1980s, Luks accepted an executive-director position at the Institute for the Advancement of Health, an organization that highlighted connections between people's health and their life choices. While there, he read papers suggesting that people who worked closely with others had better health than people who spent more time alone. This seemed to tally with his own experience, and he wondered if volunteering in particular might help foster health and well-being. He'd talked to plenty of people with compelling stories about how good their altruistic acts made them feel. One woman, a recovering alcoholic, described volunteering as like taking a drug. Another, who had multiple sclerosis, noticed that her symptoms were less severe when she worked on a crime-prevention committee.

While Luks was intrigued by the apparent connections among helping, happiness, and health, he wasn't the first to propose their existence. Helping others to boost mental outlook has a rich and storied heritage going back to the 1800s, when asylums prescribed "moral treatment" that often involved training patients to assist others in the community. In the 1960s, the social psychologist Frank Riessman published an article in the journal *Social Work* arguing for a concept he called "helper therapy." He had noticed that in self-help groups, people seemed to derive substantial benefit from providing support to others in the group. The act of helping, Riessman noted, might benefit the helper even more than the person being helped.

Buoyed by colleagues' encouragement and the inspiring stories he'd heard, Luks resolved to study the possible volunteering and well-being connection more broadly. Working with the biopsychologist Howard Andrews of the New York State Psychiatric Institute, he put together a seventeen-question survey designed to ferret out possible connections between volunteering activities and the volunteer's overall level of well-being. Luks and Andrews sent their anonymous survey to more than three thousand volunteers around the country, people involved in a dizzying range of unpaid efforts: assistance to

AIDS patients, homeless outreach, hospital volunteers, and youth mentors, just to kick off the list. After the thousands of completed surveys made their way back, Andrews did a computerized analysis of the data.

Many volunteers, Luks and Andrews found, reported distinctive sensations during and after volunteering. A whopping 95 percent of survey respondents reported a pleasurable physical sensation associated with helping others—a feeling Luks began referring to as the "helper's high." Volunteers testified that inner warmth and a pronounced energy spike were characteristic qualities of this high. Luks also learned that frequent volunteers were more likely to report lower levels of pain and to enjoy higher overall well-being. The beneficial effects on wellness seemed to be associated with the frequency of helping: People who helped others every week on a personal basis were ten times more likely to report good health than those who volunteered only once a year.

Some of the survey respondents expanded on their answers by writing comments at the bottom of the form about how they felt when volunteering. "I got very excited for the individuals I helped," one respondent wrote. ". . . I am a runner, and I felt I ran better than ever before. I felt very strong physically. Almost like nothing could conquer me. You want so much to help others, and when you do and see their reactions, you feel so good inside that it makes you explode with energy."

Luks published his results in a comprehensive report for *Psychology Today* and in his book *The Healing Power of Doing Good*, but it would take years more before a variety of other studies confirmed the strength of the connection between altruism and well-being. In 1999, the behavioral medicine specialist Carolyn Schwartz, then at the University of Massachusetts, and her colleagues divided multiple sclerosis patients into two groups and had members of one group call members of the other regularly to provide them with emotional support. After tracking the two groups for three years, Schwartz found that the helpers—the people in the phone-call group—reported profound improvements in their self-worth and their moods. "These people seemed to be blossoming," Schwartz says. "They talked about how helping other people transformed their experience of multiple sclerosis from something that victimized them to something that enabled them to be a positive force in the world."

A similar Brown University study found that Alcoholics Anonymous members who were helping other addicts by providing them with emotional and moral support were less likely to have relapsed a year after their initial treatment (calling to mind a Norman Schwarzkopf quote: "You can't help someone get up a hill without getting closer to the top yourself"). And in a 2010 survey of more than 4,500 volunteers, 89 percent—nearly 9 in 10—stated that volunteering improved their sense of well-being, while a sizable majority reported that it lowered their stress levels and enhanced their sense of purpose in life. This connection appears to hold true regardless of culture: In a 2012 study of older Maori and non-Maori in New Zealand, those who volunteered more often scored higher on happiness measures.

In best-case scenarios, regular helping may even help stave off an early death. Analyzing data from more than seven thousand respondents collected for the government's Longitudinal Study of Aging, the researchers Alex Harris and Carl Thoresen found that frequent volunteers had a 19 percent lower mortality risk than people who never volunteered when the subjects' level of social support was taken into account. That means volunteering is associated with longer survival independent of the advantages social ties provide. Even more dramatically, when University of Michigan researchers studied 423 older couples who were followed for five years, those who helped others were nearly 60 percent less likely to die during the study period than those who never helped.

While many survey studies have found more or less strong associations between helping and happiness, the University of California, Riverside, psychologist Sonja Lyubomirsky wanted to test the connection in a real-world setting. She asked students to carry out five "random acts of kindness" of their choice every week for six weeks—they could choose anything that benefited others, from making a homeless person a meal to helping a kid with a school assignment. The subjects experienced higher levels of happiness than controls when they performed all five kind acts in one day, suggesting that the well-being boost is pronounced when people help often.

Interestingly, though, students who spaced the kind acts out, performing them on different days, *didn't* experience the same happiness boost. Lyubomirsky's work suggests altruistic acts may need to be frequent in order to confer a lasting change in well-being. With isolated acts of helping, says the London School of Economics social scientist Francesca Borgonovi, "it could be there's a very short—narrowly defined in time and space—bump in happiness that doesn't shift your [overall] happiness in any meaningful way."

On balance, though, being generous boosts your mood and health because it strengthens your sense that you're really doing something significant. The social psychologist Sara Konrath of the University of Michigan notes that helping others may signal our bodies to release pleasurable chemicals such as oxytocin. The boost we get from helping may also mute our stress response, causing us to release fewer jarring stress hormones such as cortisol and norepinephrine.

Evolutionary psychology suggests there are good reasons those chemical responses exist. Stephen Post, director of the Center for Medical Humanities, Compassionate Care, and Bioethics at Stony Brook University and author of *The Hidden Gifts of Helping*, points out that it may make reproductive sense for us to derive pleasure and well-being from helping other people. "Evolution suggests that human nature evolved emotionally and behaviorally in a manner that confers health benefits to benevolent love and helping behaviors," he wrote in a 2008 *Psychology Today* column. "We seem to prosper under the canopy of positive emotions."

What kinds of helping are most likely to lead to lasting satisfaction? In general, it's the activities that allow us to spend quality time with the people we're helping. For the biggest mood boost, Jonathan Haidt, a New York University psychologist and author of *The Happiness Hypothesis* and *The Righteous Mind*, has recommended performing good deeds that bolster your relationships with others.

A casual experiment I did some time ago, recording how I felt after carrying out various unselfish acts, seems to support this theory. I enjoyed writing a letter to an old French teacher who'd had a big impact on my life, knowing she'd appreciate my gratitude, but feeding a vending machine so the next buyer would get a free treat barely boosted my spirits at all. In the real world, the acts of kindness that made me happiest involved building relationships. "There's a benefit— you can think of it as distraction, but I think it's bigger than that," Schwartz says. "You're creating more and more invisible lines of connection in the world, so you don't feel as isolated and alienated. When you're helpful and kind in the greater world, you're going to start to experience community in many other places."

While I've always liked the utilitarian appeal of "the greatest good for the greatest number"—it seems more sensible to write an article for an audience of five thousand than to tutor a disadvantaged student for an afternoon—Schwartz's advice rings true. There's a sense of satisfaction I get from mentoring individual high school kids that I don't get from churning out stories on my laptop. James Frank, a longtime volunteer with the Bay Area's branch of Big Brothers Big Sisters, feels the same way about the relationship he's built with his young mentee, Elijah. "When I started with Elijah, they tell you you have to hang out twice a month for an hour, but you get addicted right away," he says. "I see the results of what I do through every interaction I have with him. I feel like by doing what I'm doing, I'm giving this kid a leg up, and that makes me feel better about walking down the street." In practice, though, many of us don't seek out such interpersonal helping opportunities: It's a lot easier to write a check to charity than to devote a weekend afternoon to a neighborhood fund-raiser. Our immediate interest in efficiency often trumps our long-term interest in building and maintaining social support through helping.

Despite the mood and health benefits to be gained from helping, it might actually be counterproductive to help exclusively with those benefits in mind. Konrath, the Stony Brook University social scientist Stephanie Brown, and their colleagues found that the people who experienced the most significant longevity benefits from helping were those with the unselfish goal of helping others for its own sake. People who volunteered with self-interested motives—in hopes of escaping from their own troubles or feeling better about themselves, for instance—had a mortality risk similar to those who didn't volunteer at all.

Some might interpret this to mean the altruism-and-well-being connection doesn't hold up, but Schwartz disagrees. "To do the helping behavior because you want to get healthier—it's a little messed up to do it for that reason. I would much rather encourage people to do it because it makes the world a better place." It's most constructive not to think of the "helper's high" as an end in itself, but as a fringe benefit you reap because you concerned yourself with someone else's welfare. While you likely *will* feel better as a result of helping, viewing your helping efforts chiefly as a self-improvement program might interfere with one source of good health and feelings: By helping unselfishly, you're setting aside anxious self-focus to attend to the needs of the world at large.

That said, few people boast absolutely pure motives when it comes to helping. Many people continue to do it, at least in part, because they come to enjoy it so much. Nonprofit organizations depend on this long-term effect in order to keep volunteers in the fold. Luks claims the high he experiences as a helper is different in some aspects from anything else, including the lift he gets from spending time with his own family. He speaks of himself as someone who's "hooked" on helping, though he never loses sight of the interests of the person he's trying to assist. "People argue that of course we're benefiting ourselves, so it's not altruism. But the equation has two ingredients. If I'm helping someone *and* I feel good, how does that make me not a helper?"

What about heroism in a riskier or more death-defying sense—does *that* lead to happiness as well? While this question has not yet been studied in detail, it stands to reason that heroism's effects on mood and health may be different—and more complicated—than the documented well-being boost that altruism provides. For one thing, heroes who assume substantial risk must often buck social norms or face personal peril in order to achieve their objectives, which could in theory lead to great unhappiness. Dave Hartsock, the skydiving instructor who loves being active in the great outdoors, has been consigned to a motorized chair as a result of his heroic feats. On the other hand, there's the potential happiness upside of knowing you've saved someone's life or demonstrated moral courage when it most counted. Hartsock says he gets great satisfaction from the choice he made to save Shirley Dygert, despite his subsequent injuries, and he insists he wouldn't have done things any other way.

While volunteering typically involves lesser sacrifice than headline-making heroic acts, it too involves some degree of difficulty and inconvenience, sometimes so much so that it crosses the divide into no-holds-barred heroism. Somewhat counterintuitively, seasoned altruists often continue to take long-term joy in their work by reminding themselves that the good to which they're contributing is far larger than their own momentary well-being. "I think, 'I cannot do one more thing,' then I picture the face of a Rwandan woman who went through a genocide," says Victoria Trabosh, president of the Itafari Foundation, which supplies business microloans and schooling fees to Rwandans in the aftermath of the ethnic conflict that killed hundreds of thousands. "If she can do that, you honestly begin to see, 'I can do this.'"

Given the long-term health and happiness benefits in the offing for dedicated volunteers, why do so many nonprofit organizations fall short when it comes to finding and keeping them? In Luks's view, it's partially because people aren't yet aware enough of helping's benefits to make it a serious priority. "Everyone says that's the biggest reason, time," he muses between bites of steamed veggies. He mentions a group of doctors he plans to speak with about the importance of volunteering. "Will they believe Allan Luks's talk? Will they say, 'Oh, it's true, but you know what my schedule is like'? Compliance is one of the great challenges."

Certainly, the demands of our hectic lives—and, let's face it, our own inherent laziness—often scuttle our desire to help others. When you're streaking down the freeway to a meeting that started fifteen minutes ago, you're not very likely to assist a stranded motorist standing by the side of the road, and an eighty-hour workweek doesn't leave much time for sustained volunteer commitments. It's also difficult to stay motivated when the happiness benefits aren't immediate. When the phone rings on a weekend morning and an acquaintance from work asks you to pitch in on his Habitat for Humanity project, it's a lot easier to plead illness and retreat under the covers than to drag yourself out of bed and dig out the tool belt. (I know this all too well; though I'm fully aware of the long-term well-being benefits I get from helping others, that doesn't make it any easier to wake up at 7:00 a.m. on Saturdays for volunteer meetings.) And just as some introverts dread social encounters but report feeling happier after them, many people underestimate the happiness boost volunteering will ultimately give them. "Doing something nice gives you more happiness bang for your buck," the Yale psychologist Laurie Santos says. "However, people really don't know that's true for themselves. We don't have great predictive power over what's going to reward us and what's not."

That's exactly why it's so important to be aware ahead of time of the strong connections between helping and happiness. Once you know intellectually that helping is good for your own well-being as well as good for the other person, you may be more likely to persist even if it's uncomfortable or annoying in the moment. And once you experience the ultimate benefits, you'll be more likely to stick with the helping activity you've chosen. Luks stresses that it's critical to try a variety of helping opportunities to see which ones suit you best. When two women he knew were volunteering at a nursing home, "one woman said it was a beautiful experience, and the other said, 'I don't like it because it smells.' That specific helping situation wasn't right, but it doesn't mean you can't find another."

More widespread awareness of helping's benefits may compel more people to take altruistic or heroic action, but Luks thinks significantly boosting volunteer numbers will require mobilization on a societal scale—perhaps a challenge from a prominent national politician, like John Kennedy's famous charge to Americans to serve their country. Doctors could also be instrumental, Luks says, in alerting their patients to the health benefits of helping. What's needed are professionals to explain why altruism is a potentially life-changing prescription. "It's not that you have to find proof. The question is 'How do you get people to *listen* to the proof?'"

For now, Luks hopes he can get results driving his point home one conversation at a time. Short of a society-wide revolution, he's resolved to spread the word about his life's work through casual evangelism. "I tell my friends, I say, 'You're going to live long,' and I give each of them the federal government study. You have a chance to feel better about yourself and have better health and you turn it down?" Hrostoski, too, has a simple message for people who are on the fence about getting more involved in volunteer work. "There's probably at least twenty hours in everyone's week that are a total waste of time. Make it a commitment. The benefits that you get from it are unreal." If the burgeoning field of selflessness science is any guide, your body and your mind will both thank you.

Chapter Seven
THE SCIENTIFIC SEARCH FOR ALTRUISM

t's a warm fall day at Stanford University, and since the early morning hours, the campus has been bustling with throngs of students, out-of-town visitors, researchers, and Buddhist acolytes, all eager to catch a glimpse of the Dalai Lama. But His Holiness isn't in town to air political opinions or minister to spiritual seekers— he's here to engage researchers from Stanford and elsewhere in a dialogue about the scientific roots of compassion and altruism. This dialogue is taking place in front of an enthusiastic crowd of scientists and curious members of the public.

Inside, the stage is set up like a living room. A small group of scientists are arrayed around the Dalai Lama in armchairs, and His Holiness himself sits in the middle, clad in burgundy robes, a cup of tea perched on a small table next to him. The neurosurgeon Jim Doty, founder of Stanford's Center for Compassion and Altruism Research and Education (CCARE), explains his organization's scientific mission and the Dalai Lama's personal interest in it. "Ecologic catastrophe, global warming, poverty, war, these are not external to ourselves. They are problems of the human heart. While science and technology offer great hope, until this technology is focused on afflictions of the heart, I do not believe there is hope for our species," Doty says. "Our interest is to use the remarkable tools available today to understand these complex qualities of compassion and altruism." To welcome his eminent guest, Doty presents the Dalai Lama with a baseball cap emblazoned with the CCARE logo. Smiling his ever-present Mona Lisa smile, the Dalai Lama carefully unsnaps the strap on the baseball cap and situates it on his head.

Throughout the day, each researcher presents his or her work to the Dalai Lama and the audience. The presentations cover a diverse array of topics, from the development of programs for compassion-cultivation training to the influence of emotions on decision making.

At one point, Philip Zimbardo turns to the Dalai Lama. "I want to start with a provocative, maybe challenging question," he says. "Is compassion enough in a world filled with evil? How do we go beyond compassion, which is the highest personal virtue, to heroism, which is the highest civic virtue? Do you not have to have a socially engaged compassion in order to prevent suffering?" As Zimbardo speaks, the Dalai Lama carefully unties his shoes, removes them, and folds his legs onto the chair, tucking them under his robes.

"I think this is a great place to start—this question of heroism," says Linda Darling-Hammond, a Stanford education expert sitting just a few feet from Zimbardo. "The way we learn initially is through modeling. To provide that for most people, we need to help caregivers and teachers learn to see children as whole human beings, how to tune in to what they're thinking, what they're feeling. There are curricula that are being tried all over the country. In this teaching, children are taught to be mindful of what they're feeling, to make prosocial choices that are helpful to others." She mentions a nearby school where one such curriculum is being tried.

The Dalai Lama pauses thoughtfully as his translator interprets for him. "The school in East Palo Alto that you gave as an example," he says, through the translator. "Has there been any comparative research done on the effects on the personal life by a graduate of this school versus other schools that do not have this kind of program?"

"There was a meta-analysis of two hundred schools that had put in place programs like this," Darling-Hammond says. "There was a significant decline in violence, significant increase in students' feelings of worth in themselves, significant increase in students engaging in pro-social behavior."

The Dalai Lama nods, speaking himself this time. "After five years, ten years, [tell me] what differences. Then hundred school, thousand school, can adopt additional curricula like that."

To some students and onlookers, the Dalai Lama's visit to campus might have seemed episodic, the man himself one in a line of traveling luminaries who appear on campus to impart drive-by wisdom before leaving just as quickly. But in reality, this visit was the culmination of years' worth of communications between the Buddhist leader and Stanford researchers. Recently, many of these discussions have revolved in some way or another around Jim Doty, whose tireless efforts have established CCARE as a legitimate scientific entity.

Doty, a meditation practitioner, has a way of looking at you as though you're the only person in the room. The carefully crafted sentences that flow out of him are punctuated by large, unexpected smiles, as if there's so much joy inside of him that it can't help leaking out. He's constantly interrupted by phone calls and other visitors, but none of it appears to overwhelm him. He simply surfs the wave of whatever happens to come next, hovering above it all—which seems appropriate, since he's often the tallest person in the room.

Doty grew up poor, with an alcoholic father and a bedridden mother, which often made him feel powerless over what happened to him. When he was thirteen, he learned the basics of mindfulness meditation from the mother of a local magic-store owner. Empowered by the discovery that he could use this practice to deliberately change his outlook on life, Doty threw himself wholeheartedly into whatever he did and ended up building himself into a conventionally successful person par excellence. He went to medical school at Tulane, then did a residency at the Walter Reed Army Medical Center in Washington, D.C. He eventually became a professor of neurosurgery at Stanford and the director of the neuroscience department at El Camino Hospital in Mountain View, California. He also helped develop and pioneer use of an image-guided robot that used radiation to eradicate solid tumors anywhere in the body. He amassed $75 million on paper after helming Accuray, the company that developed the robot, and lost almost all of it in the subsequent turn-of-the-century economic slump. Despite losing most of his assets, he made good on a pledge he'd already made to donate hundreds of thousands of stock options to Stanford—options the university was able to sell for millions of dollars after the market recovered. During the lean years, Doty began thinking more and more about the mysterious nature of human generosity. "I've always been fascinated that there are people in power who decide not to be generous or kind, and there are poor people who will give you their last penny," he says.

Doty's curiosity came into even sharper focus after the Dalai Lama visited Stanford in 2005 and talked with a number of different faculty members. Inspired by colleagues' reports about the Dalai Lama's visit, Doty organized a loose-knit group of researchers who shared his interest in learning more about the scientific roots of altruism. This informal venture was called Project Compassion.

The number of participants in Project Compassion grew, and Doty and others were eventually able to convince the then Stanford medical school dean Philip Pizzo to create CCARE. The center would take on as its mission not just probing the ultimate origins of compassion and altruism, but drawing on scientific findings to create a society of better, more generous, more helpful people.

When Doty met with the Dalai Lama at a conference in Seattle in the spring of 2008, he was initially awed and overwhelmed to be in the Tibetan leader's presence, but his warm, gentle demeanor put Doty at ease. The Dalai Lama told Doty he was so enthusiastic about a research organization devoted to understanding compassion that he wanted to contribute $150,000 of his personal fortune to the cause—the largest personal donation he'd ever made in the name of science. He also agreed to pay another visit to Stanford in late 2010.

CCARE officially opened its doors in 2008 and has been supporting research and community outreach ventures ever since. While much of its science is highly technical at this stage—mapping the regions of the brain that govern compassion, gauging people's performance on donation tasks in a lab setting—the center's goals are ultimately practical ones. "We want to see the effect on the person," Doty says during the Dalai Lama's Stanford visit, referring to the impact of compassion cultivation strategies. "We should be examining the impact on those around you."

"If you don't measure it and show that it improves their relationships with their children and their intimate partner, it's useless," another scientific panelist, Paul Ekman, adds. "The important thing is we change how people deal with each other."

Since Doty himself has a limited academic research background, his principal role is as an encourager and evangelist for the altruistic cause. He travels from place to place talking to large audiences; he also talks to researchers about their ideas and makes sure the most promising ones get encouragement and funding from CCARE. "Maybe I'm just a Pied Piper," he says, laughing.

While Doty was working to get CCARE off the ground, his Bay Area colleague Phil Zimbardo was starting his own related venture, the Heroic Imagination Project (HIP). Over the course of more than three decades, Zimbardo has established himself as one of the premier global authorities on the psychology of evil. With HIP, he's reshaping his insights into why ordinary people do bad things into programs that train people to resist nefarious influences and make heroic choices instead. "I should have done this thirty years ago," he tells me one late-summer morning, settling into a chair in his light-filled living room in San Francisco's Russian Hill neighborhood. He's still walking with a cane the day of our talk, having undergone surgery recently, but his schedule is already ramping up again with unprecedented speed. There are curricula to develop and flesh out, funds to raise, business partnerships to cement. Preparing to transform ordinary people into heroes, it turns out, is some of the hardest work he's ever done.

Zimbardo's improbable identity as a sculptor of heroes began to take shape more than fifty years ago. When he earned his psychology Ph.D. from Yale in 1959, the wounds the Nazi regime had inflicted on occupied Europe were still relatively fresh. So many moral questions preoccupied people in those sober postwar years: What had turned the Nazi functionary Adolf Eichmann into such a monster, coordinating schedules for trains that carried thousands of people to the gas chambers at Auschwitz? Prior to Hitler's ascent to power, he'd been a sales clerk with a seemingly innocuous personality. And what had compelled the ordinary soldiers in Einsatzgruppen units—many of them devoted husbands and fathers who wrote to their families regularly—to murder Jewish men, women, and children in cold blood?

Stanley Milgram, Zimbardo's old high school friend, supplied the possible beginnings of an explanation when he conducted a landmark experiment showing that most subjects inflicted what they believed were high-voltage electric shocks on others when an authority ordered them to do so. The study revealed that when confronted with apparent orders from a superior, people were disconcertingly willing to shove their morals into the background in order to comply. Under such circumstances, heroic action was a vanishing possibility.

Zimbardo was interested in further exploring the idea that certain situations can exert powerful influences over people that may cause them to act against their conscience. By the 1970s, he'd become a Stanford professor of psychology, and in 1971, he set up the infamous study known as the Stanford Prison Experiment. He recruited twenty-four normal college students from around the Palo Alto area and randomly assigned half of them to play "prisoners" and the other half to play "guards." He armed the guards with wooden batons, but instructed them not to harm their charges physically. The prisoners were locked in small rooms in the basement of Stanford's Jordan Hall and issued poorly fitting prison smocks.

What happened over the course of the next six days went far beyond what even Zimbardo could have imagined. The makeshift prison was relatively peaceful at first, but on the second day, the restless prisoners revolted. To reassert their authority, the guards resorted to an assortment of sadistic tactics, including forcing the prisoners to strip naked, restricting their access to the bathroom, and forcing them to perform simulated acts of sodomy. The speed and intensity with which things escalated still makes Zimbardo shake his head and gaze off into the distance. "It became a strange reality that all of us were sucked into," he says. "I can't believe what I allowed to happen."

That the experiment ended after six days at all, Zimbardo continues, was due to the heroic influence of the woman who would later become his wife. At the time, Christina Maslach had recently finished her Ph.D. at Stanford; she was a greenhorn in her field compared with Zimbardo. Nevertheless, she stepped up to tell him in no uncertain terms that what he was doing to his subjects was unethical. "She persuaded me with tears," Zimbardo says. "She said, 'I'm really concerned. I don't know who you are anymore.'"

Zimbardo decided to end the experiment the next day. He marveled at Maslach's selflessness—her willingness to make herself vulnerable to defend the well-being of the experiment's participants—and wondered why she'd spoken out when so many other people in her position would have kept mum. "Why did I not study heroism at *that* point?" he muses. The simple answer: He got distracted. The media and the public were so interested in Zimbardo's insights about the genesis of evil that he was invited to appear on one TV program after another. Meanwhile, he continued his study of situational factors that can provoke immoral behavior.

The culmination of Zimbardo's decades-long focus was the period when he wrote *The Lucifer Effect*, a book about how the pressure cooker of circumstance can give rise to evil in settings as diverse as the Abu Ghraib prison and the basement of Jordan Hall. The last chapter of the book—the only one, he now reflects, that filled him with hope—was about how to resist negative influences that can give rise to evil tendencies.

As he wrote the chapter, he found himself thinking more and more about what Maslach had done so many years ago and why. In a situation where most people would have gone along with a senior colleague's wishes, Maslach had proven uniquely willing to speak out. What allowed some people to turn a blind eye to perceived injustice, while others stepped forward to stop it—even at the risk of endangering their own well-being? "To be a big hero, you need a big opportunity. There has to be a corrupt system you're willing to oppose," he says. But he was also interested in selflessness of the more common—and less commonly acknowledged—variety: acts like speaking out against a boss's unfair treatment of an office colleague, or caring for an elderly relative when no one else is willing to take her in.

During a lecture at the TED conference in 2008, he floated the idea of using science-based principles to develop people's heroic capacity. Much to his own surprise, he received a standing ovation. "Afterward a hundred people came up to me and said, 'This is so exciting.'"

Over time, the Heroic Imagination Project began to take shape in Zimbardo's mind. Inspired by his colleagues' interest, he decided to create an organization geared toward preparing people to become their best selves in any morally-charged situation. HIP would conduct scientific research on the origins of heroism—how people define heroism, what influences compel individuals to take heroic action—but it would also design and implement curricula intended to awaken people's heroic instincts. "Our job," he says, "is 'How do you fortify the general population against the allure of the dark side?'"

After CCARE's inception, Jim Doty knew some scientists were looking at him askance. What was a *brain* surgeon doing heading a high-profile research organization like this? "It is extraordinarily strange that a major research entity at Stanford is headed by someone with no domain experience," he admits. But Doty also believes he has personal strengths that are both rare in the research community and necessary for keeping CCARE afloat. "One, I can create a vision, paint a picture of the importance of what we're trying to accomplish. The other talent I have is throwing out ideas and having experts tell me if they're worth pursuing. Sometimes fascinating ideas come out of that." It was Doty, for instance, who convinced researchers to create a reliable scale to measure compassion. "I said, 'Shouldn't there be a compassion measurement index that people agree on?' I was pooh-poohed, and then people started saying, 'We need a compassion measurement index.'"

Perhaps Doty's greatest talent, however, is that he serves as a kind of Gertrude Stein figure within the nascent science-of-altruism community, creating salons where the field's leading figures can build relationships and bounce ideas off one another. To that end, he and CCARE spearheaded a Science of Compassion conference in 2012 in Telluride, Colorado—a town so elevated that the tops of surrounding peaks often get lost in the clouds. The conference would feature presentations from emerging heavyweights of selflessness science: Phil Zimbardo, Bill Harbaugh, Richard Davidson, and dozens of others. The meeting would give these rising stars the opportunity to trade insights that might ramp up the pace and quality of altruism research. Cross-pollination, Doty hoped, would beget continued inspiration. The conference would also be open to the public, fulfilling Doty's twin goals of making his center's discoveries accessible and broadly conveying the importance and potential impact of CCARE's mission.

More than three hundred people make the trek to the mountains to attend the conference, held in the Telluride High School theater. When I step into the lobby, there isn't a tailored suit in sight; weathered T-shirts, cargo pants, and long, flowing skirts are the dominant attire for attendees and presenters alike. You can pick up brochures about Naropa University's programs in Buddhist studies, eat gluten-free cookies, or purchase CCARE T-shirts that say GOT COMPASSION? One presenter—perhaps a veteran of more traditional scientific conferences—actually apologizes for his button-down-and-tie outfit. (Doty himself, ever the bridge between worlds, is clad in a blazer, pin-striped shirt, and jeans.)

These sartorial choices reflect the tone of the presentations, which is casual, down-to-earth, and friendly. Like Oscar winners, presenters go out of their way to thank their scientific collaborators, sometimes listing more than a dozen individually. And many presenters kick off their talks with personal stories of what led them to compassion research.

But despite all the nontraditional trappings, the science being presented—the meat of the twenty-minute talks—is decidedly rigorous.

Brian Knutson of Stanford presents on areas of the brain that showed enhanced activity on fMRI scans when subjects were told to extend compassion to someone else, and the University of Oregon's Bill Harbaugh outlines his studies on brain areas activated during charitable contribution. One conference staff member remarks to me, as I wolf down a lunchtime burrito from a Telluride food truck, that he wishes the conference were "a little more metaphysical."

In fact, there are so many presentations packed into the four days of the schedule that I sense much of the scientific impact of the conference will be spread out over the days and weeks to come. There is certainly potential fodder for future collaborations here: I can easily envision some of the brain-imaging scientists, for instance, partnering up with in-the-field researchers who are piloting community interventions designed to elicit empathy and concern for others. That way, MRI scanning technology could be used more extensively to evaluate the effectiveness of real-world compassion training, not just short-term lab-based efforts to encourage generous behavior. During the conference sessions themselves, though, there's precious little opportunity to plan such cross-disciplinary ventures; most attendees are so engaged in listening to and processing the tsunami of information that it will take time before they can seriously consider how to put all of it to practical use. The synergistic breakthroughs Doty envisions will have to wait for a while—at least, until the attendees have a chance to decompress and fully process everything they've learned.

What impresses me, though, is that there's a more-than-passing attempt to focus on the practicalities of all of this research, to reflect on its implications for generations to come. The second day of the conference happens to be the day a deranged gunman named James Holmes infiltrates a showing of the Batman film *The Dark Knight Rises* in Aurora, Colorado—just a couple hundred miles away from where we sit in the high mountains, insulated from the world. After the horrific shooting, discussion at the conference soon turns to whether heightened compassion and interest in others—on the shooter's part or on the part of those around him—could have prevented such a tragedy from occurring. The question is, of course, unanswerable, but the researchers in Telluride seem to agree that understanding the genesis of compassion for our fellow human beings is key to activating it in ways that would make violent acts like the Aurora tragedy unthinkable. The immediacy of the Aurora shooting supplies an unforgettable reminder to the scientists present here—that if the kind of seismic change sought by organizations like HIP and CCARE is to be meaningful, it will happen not at the theoretical level but at the individual one. "Compassion for me means instead of getting into the impulse to condemn, get into the search for understanding," Zimbardo says as the auditorium erupts in applause. "The reason to understand is to prevent."

Having a prosocial vision is one thing, but securing the financial backing needed to carry it out is quite another. Zimbardo devotes huge amounts of time to what essentially amounts to pounding the pavement. Like the heads of ballet companies and volunteer outfits, he has to plan everything he does with an eye to courting potential donors—and that means getting the word out about his program to the stars of the Bay Area's business community. His ultimate goal is to kick fundraising into gear, of course, but also to showcase HIP to community leaders who have enough clout to champion the cause.

One typical HIP informational event, held on the Stanford campus, attracts an eclectic mix of corporate leaders and students and professors from Stanford's law and business schools. The registration table is tiled with rows of nametags crisply preprinted with attendees' names, and a lavish appetizer spread features mozzarella–cherry tomato skewers, vegetable spears, dips, pita, and cheese cubes.

I greet Zimbardo outside the auditorium a few minutes before his talk is scheduled to start. As I load my plate with veggies, he tells me— agitation creeping into his voice—that eighty people are signed up to come, and only a few dozen have shown up so far. I assure him that many are probably on their way from work, but he seems concerned that the latecomers may opt not to show up. "It's going to get to be their dinnertime," he says. At 5:53, there are about thirty or thirty-five people sitting in the auditorium seats, and by 6:00, the designated starting time, the count's up to about fifty.

Zimbardo clicks a button on his laptop and "Evil Ways" (lyrics: "You've got to change your evil ways, baby. . . .") starts playing. From there, he launches into a presentation on the detrimental effects of conformity. He cites his Stanford Prison Experiment as an example of the moral deterioration that can happen when ordinary people don't act against corrupt situational norms. The ideal strategy, he says, is to create a corporate culture that actively guards against these kinds of situations. "The best organizations create self-correcting cultures of integrity. Anything that sullies your brand is the worst thing that could happen. Every company should be rewarding internal whistle-blowing." He stops every few minutes throughout the presentation to let audience members reflect on situational influences in their own lives that might have potential to foster ethical corner-cutting. A second-year law student stands up and talks about the time he felt tempted to stretch the truth in a research report. "I knew what the law said and I knew what I wanted it to say, and they weren't the same thing."

After the presentation, Zimbardo and his colleague Brooke Deterline open the floor for a question-and-answer period. Someone asks whether ethical transgressors should ever get a second chance— whether situational circumstances should be taken into account. Deterline nods understandingly. "We don't toss the bad apple. Phil was an expert witness for one of the [Abu Ghraib] guards. He's still responsible, but there are mitigating circumstances. You give people the ability to come forward if they make a mistake."

Another woman stands up. "I just have a heads-up. You can work to make businesses based on integrity—there's financial value in them branding themselves with these heroism values. There's models out there for success that show investors there's a lot of money to be made."

Zimbardo hopes more donors and investors will eventually get on board with the audience member's philosophy—that they'll come to see that instilling a values-driven culture in companies and organizations doesn't have to mean sacrificing success and increased profits. But he acknowledges that it's going to be an uphill slog. At eighty years old, he's not getting any younger, and the constant push to promote HIP principles through fund-raisers, public talks, and seminars wears on him at times. Being a scientist comes more naturally to him than being a promoter. "We're poised to soar," he says, "but we're still held back by lack of funding."

CCARE is somewhat buffered from the kinds of financial challenges HIP faces, due to its status as an official institution at Stanford and the contributions of a number of high-profile donors. CCARE's endowments have allowed it to begin offering a full slate of compassion training courses open to public enrollment, as well as a postdoctoral research fellowship to entice recent neuroscience, psychology, and other graduates to pursue work on the origins of compassion, altruism, and empathy. Still, if Doty and his colleagues hope to keep the research results coming over the long term, they're going to need to continue their efforts to reach out to a larger audience.

Where does the field of compassion, altruism, and heroism research go from here? The science of do-gooding isn't the kind of topic that's likely to take the world by storm overnight. What people like Doty and

Zimbardo hope for is more along the lines of a grassroots revolution, school district by school district, company by company, person by person, until the concepts of everyday heroism and compassion-building reach a critical point where they catch fire.

Along the way, though, they're already encountering some resistance. CCARE, for instance, has faced questions about whether it can conduct legitimate science when some of its researchers subscribe, in whole or in part, to Buddhist principles—and when its most famous private donor is the most prominent Buddhist leader on the planet. Indeed, is it possible to do quality scientific work that's partially funded by one of the most famous religious figures in the world? Will the precepts of the religion affect the way the studies are designed?

At the 2010 Stanford presentation I attend, the Dalai Lama seems to be a kind of talisman for some of the scientists in attendance, a kind of human amulet from which they draw their strength. After the event concludes, people from the audience rush up to him so they can touch his hand or the hem of his robe. Some are crying. Compassion-science heavyweights like Jim Doty and Richard Davidson aren't shy about their reverence for the Buddhist leader, who Doty regularly refers to as "His Holiness." At the 2012 Science of Compassion conference at Telluride, the Dalai Lama's personal translator, Thupten Jinpa, gave a talk about Buddhist approaches to compassion.

It's hard to escape the conclusion that the scientists most motivated to study subjects like the link between compassion meditation and compassionate action—or, for that matter, the link between heroic-education programs and future heroic action—tend to be those who, at least privately, have already become convinced that such links may exist. "This is a field that has been populated by true believers," the Emory University scientist Charles Raison told CNN in 2010, referring to research on the effects of meditation. "Many of the people doing this research are trying to prove scientifically what they already know from experience, which is a major flaw." In fact, at the Telluride conference, many of the presenters speak about the way meditation and other Buddhist practices have changed their lives.

Most scientists try to avoid the appearance of bias: A hypothetical researcher exploring the jaw-strengthening effects of gum chewing would disclose any funding from Wrigley's and probably would not strike up public friendships with members of the Wrigley's corporate board. By contrast, some selflessness scientists in particular have openly acknowledged their relationships with the Dalai Lama, raising questions about whether these scientists could let their personal reverence for him get in the way of conducting impartial research. Davidson, for instance, has enjoyed a friendship with the Dalai Lama for years. "The Dalai Lama engages in this practice [meditation] for two hours a day," he says. "You see the power of this kind of practice when you're in his presence. You feel it palpably. It's what really just deeply touched me."

But even though establishing distance from funders is de rigueur in the scientific world, that concession to propriety hardly diminishes the strength of the connections between scientists and the organizations that bankroll their work—whether it's the government, private corporations, or drug companies. And in some ways, CCARE's work may be *less* beholden to institutional bias than your average company-funded clinical trials. Though the Dalai Lama's interest in the science of compassion and altruism initially arose out of his particular religious background, he does not fund CCARE's work in the name of promoting Buddhism, but of understanding universal human emotions and capabilities. He has also publicly stated his willingness to renounce whichever Buddhist doctrines do not stand up to scientific investigation, though how far he intends to go in making good on that statement is anyone's guess. And it's not as if Jim Doty and his colleagues are the first to benefit from religiously inspired patronage, or that such patronage is an automatic roadblock to being taken seriously. The John Templeton Foundation, established in 1987 by a rich, prominent elder in the Presbyterian Church, has distributed more than $66 million in research grants to a vast array of star-studded scientists.

As much as scientists like to talk about objectivity, about never becoming attached to particular results in advance, it often seems as though subjectivity is the spark that kindles scientific innovation. Richard Davidson, for example, might never have been moved to investigate the neural effects of meditation had he not experienced transformative change as a result of his own meditation practice. Bill Harbaugh might never have investigated the neuroeconomics of charitable giving if he hadn't had a keen interest in human welfare and in volunteering. Science that people care about, feel strongly about, cannot be performed in a vacuum, and it's common for scientists to go into their investigations with well-founded hunches about their eventual results. The ultimate test will be whether their research can make it into impartially peer-reviewed journals—and whether other, less personally invested researchers can eventually replicate it. Part of me wonders, too, whether unease with the Dalai Lama's role at CCARE isn't just an aversion to religious authorities' involvement in research. Maybe it's also a reflection of broader unease about using science as a tool to answer questions about ethics, morality, and what makes a good person—the same kinds of questions that religious thinkers and philosophers have been pondering for thousands of years.

In addition, organizations like CCARE and HIP may face future challenges simply because of the dual nature of their missions. They are simultaneously looking to define themselves as research organizations *and* as centers dedicated to specific forms of social change. While these goals aren't necessarily at cross purposes—piloting proposed behavior-changing interventions (at schools, in public classes, and elsewhere) and recording the results is an integral part of the research both organizations are performing—the parallel missions raise questions about whether it's possible to devise effective interventions when many basic questions haven't yet been answered. Zimbardo and his colleague Clint Wilkins, for instance, are already testing ways to promote heroic behavior through educational curricula, even though Zimbardo notes that little research has been done on the origins of heroism to date. Similarly, CCARE has rolled out compassion cultivation training classes well in advance of the debut of a standardized scale that measures compassion itself.

But if Zimbardo and Doty are pursuing their self-imposed missions with both barrels, they are doing so simply because of the urgency of the goals at hand: to understand and promote behavior that will make our beleaguered planet a better place to live. "At the end of the day, unless what we do has an impact on the greater society, fundamentally we're doomed," Doty tells his audience at the Telluride Science of Compassion conference. "So I would really encourage and wish that that be our end point: the action component." It remains to be seen whether fledgling research on compassion and its two natural by-products, altruism and heroism, can survive the transition from lab benches to homes, schools, and powerful institutions. But the pioneers in this field are willing to do whatever it takes to facilitate the process of finding real-world applications for selflessness research. They believe, with the potent and enviable zeal of new converts, that our survival as a civilization may depend on the success of efforts like theirs. The biggest question now is whether they can convince the rest of us to agree.

PART II
PRACTICE

Chapter Eight
HEROES IN TRAINING

The ARISE charter high school near downtown Oakland is just a few hundred feet from the train station platform where a white cop gunned down an unarmed black man named Oscar Grant in 2009, inciting a firestorm of local race riots. But at this particular moment, the ARISE students seated around an array of plastic tables aren't focused on the problems of the neighborhood. Instead, they're talking about the plight of Kitty Genovese, a white woman from New York City who was stabbed near her Queens home on March 13, 1964, at about 3:30 in the morning. Despite the presence of many witnesses in the immediate area, Genovese died after none of them came to her aid quickly enough.

"That sticks with me," says Phillip, a lanky senior. "There was a lot of people that saw, but nobody helped. They were all saying, 'Oh, someone else will help her.'"

"What phenomenon is that?" prompts Clint Wilkins, the former school principal who's leading the discussion.

Phillip pauses for a few seconds, trying to remember. "Bystander effect," he spits out.

"That's right," Wilkins says. "Nobody came to her *because* there were people watching." Scientific studies, he explains, have shown that the larger the number of bystanders who witness an emergency situation, the less likely any of them are to take action.

Alfredo, a student with unblinking hazel eyes, puts up his hand. "I think it was because *enough* people saw that she was dying. I see that, and I'm like, 'Oh, someone probably already called.' If only one person seen it, they would have called."

Wilkins nods. As a result of learning about the bystander effect, he tells his charges, they'll be able to do the right thing and step forward to help a person in distress—even if no one else does. "You've rehearsed this situation in your mind," he says.

That's the objective of the Heroic Imagination Project's pilot education program in a nutshell. While the curriculum draws on a variety of historical and scientific sources, its overarching aim is to arm students with the tools they need to become "everyday heroes," to perform self-sacrificing deeds whenever the opportunity arises. Phil Zimbardo and Wilkins have overseen testing of the program at two high schools in the Bay Area: Foothill Middle College, located in affluent Los Altos Hills, and here at ARISE. "What we're trying to do," Wilkins's assistant Lonjino Lazcano explains during the afternoon class session, "is have you guys look at yourselves and say, 'What kind of person do I want to be?'"

Like Jonas Salk's polio vaccine, HIP's strategy for buttressing students against evil involves substantial exposure to the infective agent itself. Much of its education program's curriculum is grounded in research demonstrating just how easy it is to behave passively or to succumb to sinister social pressures. The idea is that the kids' new awareness of these realities will serve as an inoculation, enabling them to surmount their own moral weaknesses by recognizing and squelching those weaknesses when they crop up. "Angel, what's that word you invented last time—'comfortability'?" Wilkins asks one student during the Wednesday classroom session. "What does it mean?"

Angel hesitates. "When people are comfortable, they want to stay in their comfort zone."

"It's like the 'smoke in the room' video where people were not knowing what to do," Marcus pipes in. When experimental subjects were alone in a room that began to fill with smoke, they typically reported the smoke to the researchers, but when they were surrounded by other people who stayed put, they usually stayed seated as well. Another lesson addressing the profound way people's social environments affect how they behave involves discussion of Zimbardo's Stanford Prison Experiment. Students learn just how quickly the assigned "guards" devolved into sadism once granted officially sanctioned authority over rebelling prisoners.

The kids seem adept at finding real-life examples of how social pressure can lead to less-than-heroic actions—such as the 2009 police shooting of Oscar Grant on the BART transit system by Johannes Mehserle, a white police officer. Phillip notes that Grant allegedly resisted arrest when Mehserle confronted him. "He [Grant] probably said, 'Here comes authority again, so I'm going to act this way.'" But he thinks good training should negate strong situational pressures that arise in the moment, saying Mehserle shouldn't get off easily just because the moral decision he made was a split-second one. "If he was trained to be in this situation, he should have known the different outcomes."

Marcus points out that Mehserle likely acted a certain way because of his uniform, just as the guards in the Stanford Prison Experiment did. "I don't think he abused it [his power], but certain things make a person think they're *over* everyone else."

"Right," Wilkins says. "You put on a uniform, sunglasses, and a hat, and what happens? You're not Marcus anymore."

The program's social psychology curriculum—the Stanford Prison Experiment, the bystander effect, Milgram, and the rest—serves as critical grounding for what is to follow. The message that just about everyone, not only born "monsters," can succumb to situational forces and commit evil or cowardly acts might seem like a gloomy indictment of the human condition. But the logical extension of this message is that everyone, not just a few predesignated saints or members of some moral elite, has the capacity to choose either evil or heroism for themselves.

That's why Wilkins believes that teaching students about where these decision points tend to appear is so essential. "You get the call to adventure, and you doubt yourself," he tells them. "You gotta deal. You gotta make a decision whether you want to get involved." Seemingly mundane factors, the evidence suggests, often determine whether or not people choose to take heroic action. In the so-called Good Samaritan experiment, for instance, subjects proved much less likely to help a person in obvious distress when they were in a hurry—even, ironically enough, when they were heading off to address an audience about the Good Samaritan parable itself. Little things, the students learn—the degree of self-focus they're feeling at a particular moment, for instance—can make all the difference in whether they're willing to put themselves on the line for someone else, which is why it's so important in critical moments to remind themselves of their commitment to serve others.

In addition to preparing inductees for specific situations where they'll be tempted to avoid selfless action, the HIP curriculum emphasizes that each person's capacity for heroism is not fixed or unchangeable. Wilkins helps students articulate their moral evolution by having them tell stories about ways they wish they would have intervened heroically in the past, then has them revise and retell the stories, describing what they would do if they were faced with a similar situation today. Students learn to talk about using a mental "pause button" to halt their automatic thought processes so they can consciously choose actions in line with their moral beliefs. As a final aid in tipping the moral balance toward heroism, participants in heroic education programs can be matched up with older mentors whose job is to encourage students to follow their moral impulses to reach out and help others, even (and especially) when it's not easy.

Presenters remind the students that heroism doesn't have to mean pulling off superhuman feats. While the course is designed to equip students to act heroically should they ever find themselves in the position to rescue someone who's fallen into an icy lake, Wilkins and Zimbardo recognize that real-life selfless acts are likely to be less jaw-dropping—and that regular practice in carrying out altruistic deeds may prove helpful in honing big-time heroic instincts. "Heroism, like altruism, is sociocentric—it's focused on other people," Zimbardo says.

To this end, some versions of HIP's developing curriculum culminate in a service project to help the students put some of the principles they've learned into action. While the project for this ARISE class will be designed by the students themselves, Wilkins guides the brainstorming to ensure that it, like the rest of the curriculum, is rooted in science—in this case, the so-called positive deviance or "bright spots" doctrine. This theory was made famous by Save the Children staff member Jerry Sternin, who was saddled with the seemingly insoluble problem of improving children's nutrition in rural Vietnam villages.

Instead of imposing a top-down solution, as many reformers would have done, Sternin looked to the "bright spots"—the small number of children in these villages who actually *were* eating well—and closely observed how their families were feeding them. Then he drew on these strategies to teach other members of the community how the problem could be solved from within. The approach worked:

Six months after the start of Sternin's program, about two-thirds of the kids in participating families were better nourished.

To encourage the kids to emulate Sternin's model, Wilkins suggests to the kids that they zero in on a problem at the school—specifically, one where the seeds of a solution might be found within the community itself. He throws out math tutoring as a possible service project. Many of the kids at ARISE have trouble with math class, he observes, but there might already be some student tutors at the school who have figured out effective ways to teach other students math principles. "We can't change the whole education system," Lazcano says, "but what we *can* do is see what's right in the situation and replicate it."

The students seem receptive to this idea. Alfredo suggests it might make sense to ask the teachers what percentage of kids actually have trouble with math—a way to make sure this project is the best use of their time. Phillip points out that they could look up state math exam scores on the California state education site to get a better read on the extent of the problem. This kind of practical, strategic planning seems very much in line with Zimbardo's accessible approach to "everyday heroism."

Wilkins is pleased. "Under our nose, we've got fifteen or twenty kids who are helping other kids," he says. "My idea is for you guys to find out what those tutors are doing, shine a light on it to really figure it out. We might have some solutions right under our nose. What I'm proposing is that this might be the unsung-hero approach to bringing change. If we could discover some of that, other schools might want to pick that up."

Not surprisingly, that's exactly what he's hoping will happen with HIP's education program: that it will spread from community to community like a meme. Wilkins and Zimbardo have plans to expand the program all over the United States—and, someday, the world. "We've got lessons that could be workshops, classes, all over the Internet," Zimbardo says.

To this end, HIP's planners have created a curriculum that teachers anywhere can use to instruct kids about the importance of intervening when it counts most. In the near future, Wilkins and Zimbardo aim to get their heroic education curriculum into many more schools and youth development organizations, reaching thousands of students across the country. Curricula tailored to students in China, Mexico, and Eastern Europe are also in the works. Eventually, Wilkins plans to turn a polished version of HIP's education curriculum into a revenue stream; any surplus funds will be funneled back into the education program. For now, though, he's relishing having an impact on one group of kids at a time, since he believes the impact of these lessons on each student's life will be profound. "When young people learn to address situations they find challenging, they are better equipped to become leaders and change agents—everyday heroes." That attitude of "everyday heroism," he and Zimbardo believe, is what will stick with them even if they never have the chance to start a social change movement or seize the controls to right an airliner in tailspin.

Zimbardo's not the only idealist hoping to fortify the general population against the dark side. Heroic and altruistic education programs are beginning to spring up around the country, their missions as diverse as their instructional methods. Some have an overt superhero theme. Some incorporate compassion meditation training to help kids generate empathy for their peers and people they meet. Others are geared expressly toward tackling particular social issues, such as bullying in schools.

What many of these programs have in common is that they face the uphill task of convincing people to take them seriously in an educational landscape where money is tight, staff members are burned out and apathetic, and instilling soft skills such as empathy takes a backseat to drilling kids for state tests. To get a heroic education venture off the ground, program leaders have to find a way to set themselves apart amid the veritable smorgasbord of enrichment curricula, pull-out programs, and new teaching methods that are forever being proposed to administrators. You say you're going to train kids to serve others and sensitize them to the needs of those different from them? Take a number behind everyone else who's promised to do the same thing—and, more often than not, failed to deliver.

Matt Langdon, a heroism educator based in Brighton, Michigan, faces this struggle every day. In 1994, he moved to the United States from his native Australia, then worked as a counselor at a YMCA camp. It was later in his career at the Y that he realized that turning kids into heroes was his life's work. The Y touted character development, not just recreation, as a priority, and Langdon admired how camp leaders aimed to impart honesty and responsibility to the kids by modeling these values themselves. That sparked a brainstorm: What if he could build on this values-based approach and take it to the next level? "I want to get kids to think of themselves as heroes and act accordingly," he says.

Langdon got to test some of his ideas during what he remembers as the "transcendent" summer of 2006, which he spent as an associate executive director at a YMCA camp in Fenton, Michigan. Before the camp started, Langdon gave a talk to all the staff and counselors at the camp about the importance of seeing themselves as potential heroes—and using that vision to instill heroic behaviors in the kids. The kids responded in dramatic fashion, he remembers, taking responsibility for their behavior, helping other kids, and expressing a desire to become true heroes in their own lives. The summer was so memorable, Langdon says, that many of the staff and counselors who were there that year have stayed in touch. "Everyone realized that they had the potential to be a hero for all those kids."

Before that, though, when Langdon had gotten up the courage to ask his employers at the Y if he could create a camp program specifically designed to inspire kids to become heroes, he was met with a flat-out no. Langdon, undaunted, decided he was going to create such an educational program himself. Ultimately, he quit his YMCA job and began designing different versions of the program for both schools and summer camps.

The curriculum Langdon has devised is constructed around exposing kids to the stories of real-life heroes; encouraging them to undertake small heroic acts every day as practice; and having them articulate and adhere to moral codes of conduct that they derive. "If you see on your wall every day that you've pledged to be courageous, it's going to enter your head when that situation comes," Langdon says. "What we're trying to influence is that moment when you see something needs to be done."

After Langdon put the finishing touches on his teaching materials, he needed to get schools interested in the program—which was, and continues to be, a hard slog. As he soon learned, he was competing with dozens upon dozens of other enrichment programs, all battling for their own share of administrative attention and funding from school districts. "It's a very competitive industry," he says. "The response of a lot of principals is to ignore it all." So far, he has been able to convince only a handful of schools to adopt versions of his curriculum, despite sending out countless e-mail missives and informational packages. "I got a box and put in a packet of information, a water bottle, et cetera. I sent thirty or forty of those, all to schools I had some kind of link to. There was zero business out of that."

While Langdon plans on persevering to get more school programs off the ground, one of his big dreams has long been to run a heroic-education camp, to go back to his YMCA roots. In 2011, he learned he would finally get that chance—a YMCA branch in northern Michigan agreed to let him run a weeklong Hero Camp in the summer. He was elated. "Having kids for a week is just incomparable as far as being able to change their outlook on life—everything they touch is related to heroism. It's a hero's journey. You're leaving your old world and going to this new world with new people."

But when I arrive in the tiny town of West Branch to look at Hero Camp, it's obvious things aren't going the way Langdon intended. To start with, there are only a few dozen campers at the entire camp this week—fewer than camp directors had hoped, likely due to the down economy and the upcoming Fourth of July holiday. Langdon and his assistants had hoped to have their own group, but due to the low numbers, the Hero Camp program has been demoted to a workshop in the evenings to introduce all the kids in the camp to heroic principles.

Understandably, Langdon isn't thrilled—but true to his heroic ethos, he's determined to soldier on. So as dinner winds down in the dining hall and kids return their trays to the kitchen, he gets busy setting up a projector and queuing up a series of digital slides. Once the food is gone and the tables are wiped off, the kids—ranging in age from primary to middle school—move over to the tables nearest the projection screen.

Langdon decides to kick things off by asking the kids to relate examples of hero-like behavior in their everyday experience. "Can you give me an example of a good little thing someone has done?" he says.

There's no response for a few seconds. One kid volunteers the name of a friend who cleaned up his area in the cabin. "Actually, all the counselors did something good because they signed up to be at camp," a small girl in pink volunteers.

"Great example," Langdon says. Next he reintroduces the concept of the Hero's Journey, using the example of Peter Parker in Spider-Man. He asks the kids to recount how Parker became a hero, using some of the hero's-journey waypoints he's described in the past.

"Peter Parker starts out at home with his aunt and uncle," one boy says.

"He's a geeky kind of guy," Langdon agrees. "So then he gets a call to adventure. What is it?"

"A spider bites him."

Langdon nods. "Yes, a spider bites him, and that changes everything." A few minutes later, he moves on, broadening the scope of his hero's-journey exploration. "An important part of the journey is that every hero has a team of friends. No hero is successful by himself. Who's helping Harry Potter?"

"Hermione and Ron," a girl in purple chimes in.

"In Greek mythology, there's a story about Jason and the Argonauts," Langdon continues. "Jason had to capture the golden fleece, but he knew he couldn't do it by himself. So he put a bunch of other people in the ship to help him. If you had to put together a team, what people would you have on your team?"

"I'd have people who were tough and smart," a red-haired boy says thoughtfully.

"He-Maaaaan!" another boy yells.

Langdon leads the kids through the exercise of choosing the right people to be on their team, passing around a worksheet with blank lines to be filled with team members' names. First, he tells them to choose a best friend, someone who will be absolutely trustworthy. Then a "cheerleader," someone who provides support.

"He-Maaaaan!" the same boy yells again.

Langdon laughs. "You can't put He-Man for every one." He warns the kids against listing people who might turn on them and sabotage their hero's journey. "Have any of you got any friends who talk about you behind your back? If you were going to go on the *Argo*, would you take that person with you?"

The point, as with nearly every aspect of the Hero Camp curriculum, is to get kids thinking of themselves as heroes, to make them believe there are really things they can do to make a difference in the world around them. Although Langdon's lessons are infused with hero terminology—he passes out buttons to the kids that say "Everyday Hero"—he shies away from playing up traditional superhero stereotypes or making the heroes he talks about seem larger than life. He wants them to see Peter Parker and Clark Kent as just ordinary people, people like themselves. "A lot of this action-hero stuff applies to you in your life," he tells the kids at the end of the lesson. "You can go up to a person who's getting bullied and ask if you can help. It can save people's lives."

The message seems to resonate with the kids, at least to a certain extent. "You know how we were talking about bullying yesterday?" an eleven-year-old named Alexis tells me the next day during open swim. "I go to a school where this girl is kind of the outcast. Sometimes I get a little mean, but I think I'm going to try to help her." Other kids chime in, saying Langdon's workshops got them thinking about becoming heroes at their schools, too.

Langdon himself, though, is a little uncertain about whether he's having a real impact on the kids. Spreading the word about a concept like Hero Camp, he points out, works best by word-of-mouth among families, and the enthusiasm needed to get a grassroots campaign going requires him to have plenty of quality time with the kids—time he feels he didn't really have during this turbulent first year. And then there's the challenge of getting others to understand the scope of his heroic vision. Becoming a hero needs to be an immersive experience, he believes, and all too often, real-world hero training can't match up to that lofty ideal.

While full-fledged heroic baptism might be out of reach for high school students and summer campers, educators and administrators are still interested in its ultimate potential as part of a broader curriculum—specifically, in how well heroic-education programs actually fulfill their goals. People like Holocaust rescuers and Medal of Honor winners are universally regarded as heroes, but what about the quieter, unsung do-gooders that make up the vast majority of the heroic population, the kind of "everyday heroes" Zimbardo, Wilkins, and Langdon are generally hoping to create? For that matter, is it possible to plot a student's or camper's moral development as if it were a line on a graph?

Despite these difficulties, the creators of heroic-education programs are forging ahead with assessments, partially in hopes of getting important decision-makers to take their curricula seriously. Just as most nonprofits can't secure state funding without proof that their programs are helping the populations they target, new educational interventions don't have a prayer of widespread adoption without evidence of efficacy to back them up. Langdon hopes to complete a detailed data-driven analysis of his program's impact soon, but for now, he's become adept at deploying compelling anecdotal stories to demonstrate its power. "A sixth grader who had just had my program was waiting for the bus after school and saw a big eighth grade girl picking on a sixth grader," he remembers. "She walked up to this girl and said, 'This is my school, too, and bullying has no part in it. You need to stop.'" In addition, one school tracked disciplinary visits to the principal's office before and after Langdon's heroic-education workshop; soon after the program was over, office visits had dropped by about 40 percent.

Given Wilkins's and Zimbardo's ambitions to spread their heroic-education curriculum from coast to coast, it made sense for them to build detailed effectiveness measures into the program from the start. Students enrolled in the programs at ARISE and Foothill Middle College took surveys before and after the program. The assessors measured the students' knowledge of a variety of concepts introduced in the program, including knowledge of the bystander effect, knowledge of people's tendencies to obey perceived authority, and knowledge of people's tendencies to conform to perceived expectations.

In general, the students who took the course scored higher on these measures than members of a comparison group that had not. These gains tended to be more pronounced at ARISE than at affluent Foothill, where more students may already have been exposed to similar concepts before the program. Students who participated in the heroic-education course also displayed a more pronounced "growth mind-set" after it, meaning they showed an enhanced ability to cope with mistakes or setbacks and learn from them. Finally—although self-reports should always be taken with a grain of salt—students reported that they were more empathetic, compassionate, reflective, and forgiving after participating in the program.

Already, though, it's obvious the curricula will need to be tailored to suit the needs of different age groups. One of Wilkins's early heroic-education initiatives—a collaboration with Foothill Middle College—involved training high school juniors and seniors in Zimbardo and Wilkins's heroic curriculum, then turning them loose to teach the curriculum to sixth graders at Redwood City's Kennedy Middle School in a ten-week-long after-school program. While the high school students at ARISE enjoyed the group discussions and videos, the sixth graders sometimes didn't, so the high-school-age teachers had to improvise, devising more hands-on activities to illustrate the concepts to their students. "We had to change our approach," says Becca Shipper, who taught in the program. Still, she thinks a tweaked version of the program should be offered to middle school students in future years. "Before you go into high school, being aware of conformity can help."

When kids come home talking in excited bursts about their heroic education classes, some parents will inevitably wonder whether hero-ism is the right concept to be championing to an audience of under-eighteens. The idea of heroic education sounds great. It promises to restore virtue to an educational environment that critics charge is devoid of moral fiber, and—for the most part—it encourages kids to value genuine selfless contribution over self-promotion.

But the crux of being a hero, at least in the traditional sense, is that it involves some kind of sacrifice—one big enough that not many peo-ple would be willing to make it. This raises a difficult question: If kids take the message of becoming heroes seriously, will heroism educators face blowback from parents incensed that their children have been arrested for civil disobedience—or have put their lives in danger try-ing to rescue a pedestrian from the path of a speeding train? It's pos-sibilities like these that have heroism expert Zeno Franco questioning whether a heroic education program for kids makes sense. "Instilling the ideal of heroism at a young age is important, but asking kids to act on it has the potential to be dangerous," he says. "Is it ethical? If you ask them to engage around the idea of heroism but diminish the idea down to where it's safe, it loses its fundamental power." Zimbardo, however, points out that young heroic aspirants can be counseled to avoid taking unnecessary risks—and that coaching kids to intervene in well-thought-out ways is a key aspect of HIP's approach. Heroism, in his view, is fundamentally about showing moral courage, and most "everyday hero" acts, like standing up to bullies, don't have to involve putting yourself in dire danger.

It's also worth asking whether teaching students about the com-mon antiheroic pitfalls our brains fall into (knuckling under to cor-rupt authorities or ignoring someone yelling for help, for instance) will actually enable them to sidestep these pitfalls in the future. The trou-ble, says the Yale psychologist Laurie Santos, is that that kind of aware-ness simply may not be enough to create lasting heroic changes in people's behavior, just as people continue to eat greasy, fatty food even when they know full well there are healthier options available. "There's little evidence that knowing about the biases makes you not succumb to them anymore," she says. "The sad thing is we really don't know if what we teach translates."

Listening to Santos, I feel a pang of recognition. I've immersed myself in research on heroism and altruism, but more often than not, I still bypass people on the street who ask for a little change. If *I* don't make the split-second decision to help someone in need, how can I expect anyone else to? I know all about the bystander effect, how the more people that are present in a particular setting, the less likely any one of them is to help. But that kind of psychological knowledge is most significant if it compels the possessor of that knowledge to help when the opportunity arises.

Only time will tell whether heroic educators can ultimately make good on their promises and transform students into lifelong heroes. Frustratingly, the most remarkable potential results of the program, if they do materialize, probably won't end up being easily measured or even commended at all. If a HIP education program graduate someday ends up leaving a lucrative career to start a nonprofit advocating for some important but underrecognized cause—exactly the kind of self-lessness Zimbardo is trying to foster—will HIP ever be acknowledged as the spark that gave rise to that effort? Just as the best teachers have little direct evidence of their own effectiveness, if a program's results cannot be easily described within months of its completion, its true value may remain underappreciated.

It's clear that the whole concept of heroic education, as Zimbardo and Langdon are among the first to acknowledge, is a work in progress. Still, they're content with where things currently stand: They know that scientific investigation, like moral development itself, is an ongoing process—one that seldom yields immediate results.

The HIP youth participants appreciate this intuitively. They talk about heroic education as if it were knight training, a kind of essential preparation for the morally charged dilemmas life will eventually hurl at them. "When something's not happening," Phillip says during the after-school session at ARISE, "you've got to be like a catalyst, make a move." Zimbardo hopes that the more people HIP prepares to initiate this kind of heroic change, the more others will feel inspired to stand up and follow. His vision may be an ambitious one, but he persists in his belief that HIP's trainees are collectively capable of bringing it to fruition. "Most heroes are ordinary," he says. "It's the act of heroism that's extraordinary." But heroic educators' vision doesn't end at the schoolroom door; they also aim to instill similar moral principles in much older students. Their first targets: denizens of corporate America, land of vulture capitalism and insider trading, where taking a heroic stand against wrongdoing may involve risking your status, your professional identity, or even your livelihood.

Chapter Nine
CORPORATE HEROES

Leslie Sekerka, a professor of organizational behavior at California's Menlo College, points to one of her business ethics students. "Do you have moral character?" she says.

"I think so."

"Yes," someone else chimes in.

Sekerka nods. "I think *I've* got pretty good moral character, too, but so does almost everybody. Most people will say that they're above average in terms of their ethical or moral character."

But left to their own devices, people often begin to cut ethical corners, she says. "You start doing a few small bad things, and suddenly that doesn't seem so bad. So you do a few more. It becomes a habit to pad your expense report, saying to yourself, 'They owe me money anyway.' When we get away with something, these small acts tend to grow and are now rationalized." I remember how when Enron engaged in shady accounting practices, corruption began insidiously and mushroomed when no one was willing to speak out against it.

Tonight, Sekerka explains, the class will learn techniques they can use to maintain high moral standards at work even if they're stressed out, under time pressure, or nervous about confronting their superiors. Developed by researchers skilled at eliciting behavioral change, these strategies allow employees and managers alike to practice taking moral action in a safe environment.

The kind of reality-based rehearsal they're going to do, Sekerka tells her students, can make workers confident enough to risk standing up for the right thing in a real-world setting with real consequences. Its benefits aren't limited to those with lily-white moral histories, she says. "Moral agents do not come with a special cape in their cloakroom—they're not supermen and -women. Courage doesn't mean that you're fearless. It means you practice talking about issues that are difficult and speaking truth to power."

The corporate ethics training program being demonstrated in Sekerka's class evolved out of a seemingly unrelated venture designed to help people overcome their shyness. The psychologist Lynne Henderson had spent years developing a training program for shy people, social fitness training, which drew on cognitive-behavioral therapy principles and involved before-the-fact rehearsal; her colleague Phil Zimbardo was a consultant on the venture. Shy people would practice role-playing interpersonal situations that unsettled them in hopes that getting comfortable with the give-and-take of conversation would make them less apprehensive about engaging in it.

After Zimbardo turned his lens on heroism years later, Henderson's daughter, Brooke Deterline, then working for the Heroic Imagination Project, asked her mom to come on board to help develop a corporate heroism program. "You know," Deterline said, "we could use the social fitness model." Eventually, Henderson and Deterline's program spun off from HIP to become a separate entity called Courageous Leadership. The program is based on the theory that strategies Henderson uses to bring shy people out of their shells can also be used to empower employees anxious about raising ethical concerns to their superiors. The degree of apprehension seemed like it could be similar. Shy people fear being laughed at or socially ostracized, while would-be whistle-blowers fear losing their jobs, being blackballed in their industry—or worse.

Henderson and Deterline are pioneering a modified version of social fitness training with the goal of instilling whistle-blowing instincts in corporate employees. Piloted under the radar at Google and in various academic settings, Courageous Leadership's corporate initiatives involve a kind of retraining in which participants practice asserting themselves in mock situations similar to those they might encounter in real life.

The model's initial goal is to help people identify the thoughts that hold them back from taking moral action—things like "I might get fired if I out Jeff for his weaselly accounting practices" or "If I call Lisa out for her mistreatment of Elaine, everyone else will turn on me." Afterward they practice challenging these initial assumptions to arrive at a more accurate take on the risk they run by speaking out.

The program's ultimate objective is to help employees get accustomed to the kind of very real pressure they're going to face when taking a moral stand—and to give them firsthand practice in facing that pressure. "If you can practice a particular skill, it's easier to demonstrate that skill when you're nervous," Henderson says. "You've got some feeling of self-efficacy because you've done it before." Moral assertiveness, her theory goes, isn't a "you have it or you don't" quality, but an acquired skill that can be improved through deliberate repetition.

Deterline knows firsthand just how easy it can be to let your moral guard down in a corporate setting, because she once worked at a firm where the CEO was known for being loose-lipped about divulging nonpublic information to people outside the company. When she got a call from an independent portfolio manager who claimed the CEO had relayed more information about the firm's quarterly profits than he should have, Deterline called a meeting with the chief financial officer and other officials to discuss what to do about the situation. Instead of agreeing with Deterline that the issue needed to be brought before the board of directors, the CFO—a close friend of the CEO's—dithered. Maybe they should give things a little more time, he said, and do a little more research before acting.

Deterline was floored at his response. Everything seemed to be moving in slow motion. As the people around her nodded their heads, she thought to herself, "Am I insane?" When she thought about going along with the rest, though, a profound sense of relief flooded her. Overlooking the CEO's indiscretion would mean not having to answer angry and pointed questions. Eventually, Deterline gathered the courage to insist that the matter be brought before the board, but she was shaken by her own initial willingness to excuse an ethical lapse.

The experience convinced her as nothing else could: Corporate employees needed better coping strategies to arm themselves against ethical compromise. It was too easy to make the wrong decision without really intending to. What was needed, she and Henderson agreed, was a Suzuki-style approach to corporate heroism—the kind of incremental, practice-based approach that could turn even the most tentative participants into confident moral virtuosos. People would be more likely to risk standing up for the greater good, their thinking went, as long as they felt competent to do so.

A few minutes into the Menlo College business ethics class, Sekerka turns the floor over to Lynne Henderson, and Henderson wastes no time getting to the point. "If you've gotta have a courageous conversation, the likelihood is that you're gonna be scared," she tells the students. But the more people practice when they're stressed, she reassures them, the more likely they are to stand up for what's right when it really matters.

Henderson explains something called the Subjective Units of Distress scale—SUDS for short. It's an assessment of your own discomfort, scored in a range from 0 to 100. While everyday annoyances like dealing with a difficult customer may bump the SUDS score up by varying degrees, many people report that the thought of raising an ethical concern to a superior sends their SUDS score zooming to the top of the range. In fact, the amount of discomfort people imagine feeling can sometimes be large enough that they fail to do anything at all.

This is particularly true in a highly structured corporate or organizational setting, where loyalty to the organization and colleagues—two forces that help maintain cohesiveness—can be used to justify egregious misdeeds. In 2001, when the assistant Mike McQueary saw the Penn State football team's former defensive coordinator, Jerry Sandusky, sexually abusing a ten-year-old boy in the campus locker room, he immediately reported the incident to the team's head coach, Joe Paterno. A while later, McQueary met with the administrator Tim Curley and another official, Gary Schultz, who listened to his story. But none of the men who knew about the incident called 911 or moved to have Sandusky arrested. Instead, Sandusky was reprimanded within the organization and told that he could no longer bring kids to campus. He continued to run youth football camps in the area, exposing countless other children to possible abuse.

It's precisely this kind of moral stagnation that Henderson is hoping to forestall by teaching the social fitness model to business scholars, executives, and employees around the country. Instead of aiming to get your SUDS score soaring right off the bat, she tells the Menlo College students, it makes sense to start your moral role play with a scenario that's only a little bit uncomfortable. "You start practicing these conversations when your SUDS level is around thirty to fifty," she says. "You build gradually." The idea is to start your rehearsal at a manageable SUDS level and keep ratcheting up the intensity until you're comfortable with higher levels of distress than you were initially. That way, when you encounter a real-life situation that shoots your SUDS level up to, say, 90, you'll be prepared to take action instead of feeling trapped by your fearful thoughts.

During the role plays, Henderson will ask participants questions designed to make them question the accuracy of their initial SUDS assessment of a situation. For example, if the thought of reporting another employee for stealing gets your SUDS level revved up to pulse-pounding levels, she'll press you to explain the evidence behind your thinking and what you think the potential consequences may be. She might also ask you to picture the worst thing that could happen as a result of speaking out.

Henderson believes it's important to question your own thoughts this way because most people are apt to blow negative possibilities out of proportion. Cognitive distortions such as so-called catastrophizing ("If I say something to my boss, she'll fire me for sure") and all-or-nothing thinking ("If I can't keep this job, I'm a complete failure") are common. "You identify your automatic thoughts: 'Maybe I'll get ostracized' or 'Maybe I'll get fired,'" Henderson explains to the students. "These thoughts fall into predictable categories and you can challenge them. Then you substitute a helpful alternate response." Henderson's goal isn't to make people's mental outlook artificially rosy, but to veer them closer to reality. In questioning, she often finds participants have *over*estimated the possible negative consequences of taking a stand. Once they realize this—and work out more realistic possible consequences—they often feel more empowered, convinced the fallout won't be as dire as they initially thought. Henderson also encourages participants to use "I" statements when approaching someone (i.e., "I'm uncomfortable with that strategy" rather than "You're really cutting corners here"). That helps confronters avoid making things too personal, maximizing the odds of a peaceable outcome.

To demonstrate what she means, Henderson has her colleague Leslay Choy, an economic development expert, stand across from her in front of the room. She asks her what kind of situation she wants to role-play.

"I have a manager who was really sarcastic with a fellow employee, and I want to talk with her about it," Choy says.

"What's your SUDS level when you think about it?" Henderson asks.

"Sixty," Choy says. "My worst fear is that I'll be excluded and be her next target."

"What do you think the likelihood is that you'll be excluded and targeted?"

Choy thinks for a moment. "Maybe ten or twenty percent."

Henderson nods. "What if the worst happens? What if she did exclude you?"

Choy pauses. "It would still be worth it to me," she decides, "because I've seen people leave organizations [because of bullying], and I would feel horrible if that happened."

Now that Choy has accurately assessed the likelihood of being targeted (low) and has decided for sure that she's ready to take a stand, Sekerka is asked to play the role of Choy's unreasonable manager. "I wanted to talk to you about something I saw at the meeting the other day," Choy says, her voice wavering a little. When her fellow employee talked about a report that would be ready soon, she explains, she was disconcerted by the manager's response. "You rolled your eyes and said 'I'll believe it when I see it.' Maybe we can talk about a good way to approach him."

"Are you saying it's my problem?" Sekerka retorts.

Choy patiently explains that no, that's not what she's saying; she just thinks that her colleague is doing a really good job on the project, and she wants Sekerka to realize that and treat him more kindly and fairly.

"I hear what you're saying," Sekerka concedes. "I'd like to see where you're getting that stellar performance, and I'm not really sure who's doing what. Right now all I see is that you're a star player." After a bit more back-and-forth, the mock dialogue ends on a conciliatory note, with Sekerka and Choy arranging a meeting with the colleague in question so he'll have a chance to explain and justify his contributions. Just as Henderson predicted, the consequences Choy faced in standing up for her co-worker were not nearly as bad as she feared.

After the role play, Henderson asks Sekerka what it was about Choy's defusing strategy that worked for her. "The last thing I heard was 'Let's have a meeting and negotiate this,'" Sekerka says. She turns to Choy. "You were patient, you held your ground and you didn't waver. You didn't step away."

"Is there anything I could have done to get your defenses down more quickly?" Choy asks Sekerka.

"No, I think you were quite effective."

"You don't learn this overnight," Henderson reassures the student onlookers, who are beginning to look a little goggle-eyed at the prospect of engaging in these role plays themselves. "When we go into corporations, it takes a while to get this kind of thing down. We're trying to figure out how fast people can learn this."

Role-playing intimidating situations to get comfortable with them, giving bravery and heroism room to emerge, sounds like a good idea in the abstract. But how well does this training strategy actually pan out? It's too early to evaluate the Courageous Leadership program's success definitively, since pilot programs have involved fairly small numbers of participants. Anecdotally, though, dozens of people have testified to the value of the sessions. "I left for a meeting during the session and was immediately able to apply supportive statements and question my negative thoughts in a director-level one-on-one," one participant told the evaluators. "I want to die with gratitude. The examples that were drawn out were great." Henderson thinks the program is making a difference in coaxing employees to confront ethics violators. "We did an intervention recently," she says, "where people were telling us by the end of the day, 'I did it on the spot.'"

It helps that Henderson has years of experience using the social fitness model to embolden shy people to engage in social situations. Those long-term trials have indeed demonstrated that having people role-play a particular pressure-packed situation helps them feel more equipped to deal with similar situations in the future. Groups of shy people who have undergone social fitness training for a six-month period, for instance, show lower levels of negative self-evaluation and social distress on psychological scales than they did at the start of the program. In general, recipients of social fitness training gradually find that situations that used to distress them greatly aren't as bad as they feared—that, in fact, they can weather them and emerge with their lives (and, in Courageous Leadership, their highest ethical values) intact. "You want as much as possible for people to practice in a graduated way that they can stay in a moderated range," Henderson says. "You want to have them say, 'Yes, as I get some mastery here, my SUDS level *does* drop.'"

In her own studies, Sekerka has found that moral fortitude is not an either/or—a quality you do or don't have—but a muscle that can be exercised and strengthened. People high in what she calls "professional moral courage," she's found, possess some key critical skills. They are adept at recognizing their own emotions and using that knowledge to their advantage in resolving the situation. Instead of reacting right away, they reflectively pause to determine what action they should take. They refrain from pursuing their own self-interests in the situation. And—perhaps most important—they have practiced the process of moral decision-making, much as runners might train for a marathon, so that they are prepared to respond ethically even in awkward or high-stakes situations. "You are what your habits are," Sekerka says. "Virtuousness doesn't just land on you. You have to exercise it."

It's not enough, Sekerka is convinced, just to know the ethical rules. To actually *do* something heroic, you have to be willing to put ethical principles into practice despite full knowledge of the adverse consequences you could suffer. "You want to be rewarded for doing the right thing. But in fact, you *may* get in trouble, you may lose social status." Still, she feels that the benefits of getting engaged outweigh the difficulties. "People who exercise moral courage say they can sleep better at night—they understand that doing the right thing doesn't necessarily make you popular." To help people exercise their moral capabilities, Sekerka—who is working on a book called *Ethics Training in Action*—has developed workshops to train employees in what she calls "balanced experiential inquiry." Employees identify specific ethical challenges they have faced at work: being pressured by a boss to doctor company records, for instance, or witnessing another employee being mistreated by his or her superior. They're asked to reflect on what they did about the situation. Then—guided by a facilitator—they share the dilemma with a partner and discuss what allowed them to take moral action or what blocked them from it, giving them an opportunity to consider whether there was something about the organization or the circumstances that influenced their behavior. Finally, both partners describe what they have discussed and learned to the rest of the group, which ideally helps establish shared moral values within the corporate community.

The moral dialogues that play out in these workshops can be

stressful, Sekerka admits. People tend to get testy when they're challenged about their ethical decision-making, and they may get angry or frustrated with some of the other participants. But in a way, that's precisely the point. When these situations arise, the facilitator can remind the workshop-goers that this is exactly the kind of discomfort they may experience when facing a morally challenging situation in real life. In postworkshop surveys, people report feeling fewer negative emotions when they contemplate taking difficult moral actions in the future, and they also state that getting praise from others is less important in guiding the moral decisions they make.

Based on what researchers know about how new neural pathways and default behaviors are laid down, corporate heroism programs that adopt a group-centered, rehearsal- or reflection-based approach are on the right track, says Mary Gentile, a former ethics instructor at Harvard Business School and a member of HIP's advisory council. "This is a developmental model where you learn the skills—you work together as a team so you practice them," she says. "You have a peer network where people are coming up with an action plan that's effective, figuring out together how to be influential and persuasive. You're practicing this moral muscle memory."

Finally, Henderson calls for volunteers from the class to name ethical dilemmas they've faced in their own lives. One guy stands up and explains that when he was at Babies R Us recently, he saw another customer screaming at his very pregnant wife, "Hurry the f— up!" and felt uncomfortable. He wanted to step in, defuse the situation, and stand up for the wife, but he left the store without directly confronting the man. He says that when he thinks about getting involved in a situation like this, he gets very stressed out—his SUDS level heads up fairly high.

Henderson suggests that the group role-play the situation as if it hadn't yet happened and there was still a chance for the student to make a different decision about intervening. "What's your worst fear of all?" she asks the student, to kick off the discussion. He says he has an old head injury that he's worried might get aggravated if the husband decks him. He and Henderson talk about some of the other things he's afraid of, as well as cognitive distortions that might lead him to exaggerate the possible risks he faces.

After the student has chosen other classmates to play various roles in the skit (the pregnant woman, her husband), Henderson turns to the participants still in their seats. "Would people be willing to ask him questions to help him challenge his negative thoughts? Who wants to ask the first question?"

"Do you know for certain that he'll hit you?" one student asks.

"There's a dent in my forehead," the Babies R Us guy says, laughing a little, "so he'll see my weak spot."

"Did any of us see the dent in his forehead?" Henderson says. "I didn't see it."

"He probably wouldn't hit me in the forehead," the student concedes. "He'll probably hit me somewhere else."

"How likely?" Henderson presses.

"Maybe fifty percent."

"So we're down to chance. It's only chance that he'll hit you in the forehead," Henderson says. "Say that you want to do this. What is a self-supporting thing you can say to yourself?"

He thinks for a moment. "Go in expecting the worst, hope for the best."

"How could you protect yourself?" Henderson continues. "Say he starts to swing at you. What would you do?"

"I don't know."

"Get somebody to go with you," Henderson suggests. "Say, 'I want to intervene, but I'm afraid this guy is going to hit me. Will you come with me?'"

After some more back-and-forth, the student and Henderson agree on a specific strategy: He's going to approach the man and explain calmly that he feels uncomfortable with the way he's talking to his wife. "What's your SUDS level right now?" Henderson asks.

"Thirty," the student answers. "I feel more calm, like I'm going to walk away from the situation."

With the preliminary work done, the role-play swings into action. Calmly, the intervening student approaches the "husband" and tells him he'd appreciate it if he talked more nicely to his wife. The "husband" seems taken aback at first, but is cordial, and eventually agrees to treat his wife more kindly—no physical confrontation required. The whole class claps.

"Did you meet your goal?" Henderson asks.

"Yeah," the student replies.

"Do you want feedback?" Henderson asks the "husband" what about the confrontational stranger's approach worked for him—why he didn't blow up right away when he was called out about his behavior toward his wife.

"He was relaxed. He didn't show aggression," the husband says.

"That worked for you? So you felt like he was trying to help you?"

"Yeah."

Near the end of the class, Henderson turns to the rest of the students. "What did you find helpful about this?" she asks. "How do you think engaging in regular social fitness programs would help you have more courageous conversations?"

"The feedback, definitely," says one student.

"I think it gives you comfort with the situation," another girl says.

"It makes you ready for it," someone else pipes in. "It's less scary."

The way the student with the Babies R Us dilemma responded is the way Henderson says she's seen dozens of corporate professionals react to ethical role-playing. Confronted with concrete, logical input that makes their worst fears seem not quite so daunting or less likely to materialize, most people report a significant drop in their distress levels. While they are still aware that they could face adverse consequences for taking a moral stand, these consequences no longer seem to loom quite as large.

The role plays Henderson leads also seem to bring the participants back to a less-biased assessment of the kinds of moral lapses that should not be tolerated. In the rarefied world of a business organization—particularly one where there's an almost cult-like devotion to upper management—it's easy to internalize a moral code that the rest of the world would immediately recognize as skewed. But when many employees from a single company participate in these workshops together, two organizational dynamics ideally start to develop: a sense that the company truly expects high ethical standards from its employees, and a sense that should an employee need to out someone who is behaving unethically, the community will support the whistle-blower.

Henderson and Deterline's long-term goal is to take their corporate curriculum to companies other than Google—and eventually, to see the corporate-heroism concept blossom from something presented in a workshop to something that's part of the very grounding of each institution. "If we can do follow-on work," Henderson says, "we can make more and more of a difference."

Will these kinds of role plays and seminars ultimately help foster corporate cultures of integrity and social heroism? While the initial evidence looks promising, the programs' efficacy will depend on how well rehearsal and reflection translate to performance—on whether students and employees can draw upon lessons they've learned in workshops to muster up moral courage when real-world pressure is on.

As Henderson reminds us, what matters in situations calling for moral assertiveness is not whether you feel perfectly assured in the moment, but whether you ultimately decide to take action. "Don't worry about self-confidence," she urges. "*Do it.*" And if you're seeking like-minded compatriots who are committed to putting their heroic principles into practice, chances are, there are a few closer by than you think. Some might be clad in business suits, some in habits and white collars, but others—in a nod to their comic-book role models—might be sporting face masks, larger-than-life superhero logos, and blue Spandex tights.

Chapter Ten
REAL-LIFE SUPERHEROES

We are Real Life Superheroes.
We follow and uphold the law.
We fight for what is right.
We help those in need.
We are role models.
We will be positive and inspirational.
We hold ourselves to a higher standard.
Through our actions we will create a better, brighter tomorrow.

—REAL LIFE SUPERHEROES CREED

haim Lazaros is getting anxious. It's the day of the Superheroes Anonymous annual meeting in New York City, and there's still a lot that needs to be done before the public starts to arrive. Pizzas need to be ordered for lunch. The Etsy sellers peddling their hero-inspired merchandise (metallic goggles and Superman-logo earrings) need to finish setting their wares out on the tables near the entrance. Fabric, glue, glue guns, and ribbons must be stacked on crafting tables at the back of the room so new conference-goers will be able to make their own superhero costumes. Finally, there's a TV camera crew to be tended to, with a boom mic the length of a vaulting pole. Dressed in a getup inspired by the Spirit and the Green Hornet—a black vest, a crisp white shirt, a black tie, and a black mask—Lazaros is a quicksilver vision as he darts from one side of the loft space to the other to consult with his superhero colleagues. Most of the time, Lazaros goes by Chaim, but at Superheroes Anonymous events, he's "Life," his heroic alter ego and the literal translation of his Hebrew name.

Life might seem stressed right now, but he's also more excited than he's been all year. This conference represents the culmination of what he's built his life around for the past few years. When Life was a film student at Columbia, he and his friend Ben Goldman heard about people who dressed in superhero costumes and went out on regular "patrols" to help the community. The concept grabbed him, and he and Goldman decided to make a documentary about these so-called real-life superheroes. They didn't have a lot of money to make the movie, but they opted to forge on anyway to see how far they could get. Life wanted the lone-wolf superheroes he'd spoken with to have a chance to meet one another, so in 2007, he organized the first Super-heroes Anonymous meeting, inviting all the real-life superheroes he could find to convene in person in New York City's Times Square. "I brought them together," he says. "I lost fifteen pounds killing myself to make this event."

Life's planned documentary project was eventually postponed, but after he met so many real-life heroes in person, his outlook was altered. He felt a growing desire to do something heroic in his own life—to deliberately go out on patrol to help the homeless people he saw around the city every day. When he stuffed his bag with granola bars to pass out to people on the streets, many thanked him. But sometimes, when he stuck around long enough to strike up a conversation, they asked for something other than food: toiletries, soap, warm clothing. Soup kitchens were plentiful in the city, they explained, but places to get other necessities were few and far between. A few times, Life served as a "decoy homeless person," hanging out on the streets of New York to help the city determine whether it was getting an accurate count of its homeless. He learned exactly what it was like to shiver on the hard pavement, not knowing whether someone would try to steal his belongings.

As Life continued his homeless patrols, he got to know just where people were sure to be waiting for him, and he got the contents of his plastic-baggie care packages down to a science: a warm pair of socks to protect people from the cold, a granola bar to fill their stomachs, a tiny hotel shampoo to help them get clean. All the while, he kept his focus on developing a New York City–based collective of real-life superheroes so he and his colleagues could encourage one another in their heroic efforts and bring interested novice heroes into their real-life Justice League. The costume Life is wearing today—somewhat out of the ordinary, but not unusual enough to draw stares—seems tailored to help him move fluidly between the two identities he needs to maintain this weekend: real-life superhero and unobtrusive behind-the-scenes organizer. "It's kind of a very classic superhero look, but it's utilitarian—I can move with it," he says. "It's iconic, but I can easily melt back into the crowd."

While scientists are studying the origins of heroism and altruism in MRI scanners, surveys, and experiments, these self-styled superheroes are as close as it gets to real-world guinea pigs. They're challenging themselves on a daily basis to become better people—they're living out exactly the kind of behavior heroism researchers aim to understand and encourage.

So what motivates Life and his compatriots to do what they do? Chatting with the group's regulars proves there are as many variants as there are real-life superheroes themselves. It's immediately clear, though, that assuming a larger-than-life role of their choosing allows these heroic aspirants to feel more in control of their personal destiny. Nearly all the real-life superheroes I talk to specifically mention the satisfaction that comes with taking matters into their own hands instead of trying to affect change through the bureaucracy of a larger organization. "It's great if you want to volunteer at a shelter, but some people might say, 'Oh, I have to have all those screening tests,'" Life says.

When real-life superheroes go on homeless patrols or crime-stopping missions, they don't have to wonder whether some charity or volunteer organization will put their money and time to good use. They thrive on immediate, clear-cut feedback from the people they serve—whether it's proclamations of gratitude from the homeless or would-be crime victims who tell them, "You saved my life." "I think all of us wish we could do more about certain situations. That's a natural instinct," says Zeno Franco. "It's important for people to engage and feel like they can control their destiny. These superheroes exist in our imagination, on the silver screen, and all of a sudden, this group of people is saying, 'Why can't we be that?' That's really powerful." Being a real-life superhero requires a hefty dose of ego—I don't meet any movement insiders who'd qualify as modest or shy—but the University of Winnipeg heroism expert Jeremy Frimer admires how the heroes have managed to transmute their power-loving instincts into selfless service. "On one hand, they probably love being in a position of control. But they've found a way to do it that's prosocial and consistent with the role they want to play in society."

Life says the group of real-life superheroes is more male than female, and perhaps that's because traditional superhero role models

(Batman, Superman, Spider-Man) are predominantly male as well. Still, the women involved in the movement are just as enthusiastic as their male counterparts. There's Prowler, for instance, the long-haired hero in triangular ears and black spandex who explains to me that she's frustrated by her efforts to get involved in traditional do-gooder organizations. Longtime volunteers at a soup kitchen made fun of her for volunteering only on Thanksgiving, and when she tried to donate her car, the charity told her she lived too far away for them to pick it up. She decided she wanted to help more directly, and when she read in a local events magazine that Life and his crew were holding an introductory meeting for aspiring real life superheroes, she knew she had found her outlet. "I went to the meeting, and I was one of probably thirty people," she says. "I don't know what happened to everyone else, but I've stuck with Life ever since."

Like Life, Prowler goes on patrols a few times a month to distribute warm clothes and care packages to homeless people in various New York City neighborhoods. But she also has another heroic mission: rounding up food and supplies to donate to local animal shelters and walking shelter dogs. Adding this second vocation to her heroic bag of tricks, she says, inspired her Catwoman-esque hero costume. "I thought, 'Now I'm dual-purpose,' so I thought of a half-human, half-animal character."

Prowler's day job as a personal organizer provides plenty of fodder to help her fulfill her self-imposed missions, especially her quest to clothe and care for the homeless. "My clients are constantly giving me clothing, winter stuff, hotel shampoos, mouthwash samples. I just take whatever I think is appropriate for the streets. This is all from one lady," she says gleefully as she rips open a bulging white plastic garbage bag. Inside is a mother lode: sweaters, scarves, a Patagonia fleece vest. She loves the in-the-moment nature of being a real-life superhero—the way people's faces light up when they see her and the way they thank her when she gives them something they need. "I feel useful, like I'm contributing, and I'm right there to see the payoff. It's cool to get a chance to give that feels good. And it's fun to be sexy costume girl."

Then there's Shade, who goes by his pseudonym only and stands out even in a room full of costume-clad people. His gravelly voice comes through a narrow grill in the helmet that covers his entire head and face, and black armor plates cover so much of his body that barely a square inch of skin is showing.

Growing up in the Bronx, Shade decided he wanted to try to do something to protect innocent people in his neighborhood. For years, he has gone out on patrol regularly. When he does, he typically wears some version of his costume. "People will yell out, 'Zombie Apocalypse!' and stuff, but you just brush it off." What he's looking for are crimes in progress that he might be able to stop. "The first crime was a mugging," he says. "I see someone slam someone else against a wall, and he has a knife. I say, 'Hey, what's going on?' and he runs away." Putting his own life at risk to protect people doesn't bother him, but he's serious about guarding his identity. He doesn't want anyone to find out who he really is—in part because he wants the focus to be on his actions, but also because he thinks that if he were outed, his family and friends would mock his earnest crime-fighting efforts. "I won't hear the end of it."

While Shade and I are talking, people start to mosey in from the streets. I've been expecting a frenzied atmosphere, something like Comic-Con, but the loft space doesn't feel crowded at all—there are maybe a few dozen people in attendance. They sit on the couches and folding chairs in twos and threes, talking about what brought them to the conference. Some are friends of the real-life superhero regulars, while others found out about the event online.

The first phase of our superhero initiation, Life announces, will be choosing an identity, much as converts often choose a new name to accompany their baptism. Guests paw through bolts of fabric (tulle, spandex, and comic-book themed), trim (braided and metallic), and masks (black and white) so that they can create their own superhero costumes.

After some thought, I opt to become Scribbler, a writer-hero who brings people together through the power of words. I choose a fabric with comic-book panels printed on it, cut it into a bolero-length cape, and punch a few holes at the top of the cape so I can weave a piece of satin cord through to tie it closed. Seeing me wearing the makeshift cape, one of the TV cameramen zeroes in on me. "Could you run around a little so the cape flies out behind you?" he says. I comply, cringing a little. The Superwoman shtick seems wrong, somehow: I picture writer-heroes perched perpetually in front of their laptops.

As the neophyte heroes assemble their costumes, passing the dripping glue gun back and forth, the seasoned superheroes buzz around the tables helping them refine their heroic identities. "So what's your deal?" Prowler says to a woman named Sara who's carefully cutting out a V-shaped piece of red fabric. She chose the color, she says, because it reminds her of Wonder Woman.

"I don't know." Sara hesitates.

"I had one girl who was really into science, and she wanted to expand herself, so we made her an amoeba," Prowler says, rolling a sheet of batting around curtain wire to make herself a new cat tail. "Do you have a population you want to serve?"

Sara starts talking about the seven-year-old Philippine boy she's sponsoring through Children International. For $22 a month, she's supplying him with the basic necessities of life, including food, medicine, and education. He sends her letters, and she writes back to him. She's interested in graduate programs in international relations, too. She likes the idea of doing homeless outreach with Prowler and Life, but she also likes the idea of reaching out to an even larger population.

"It has to be something 'world' or 'globe,'" Prowler muses. "Globo?"

This identity-conferring ritual is one the real-life superheroes carry out regularly, holding costume-creation workshops for interested initiates. Putting the finishing touches on my costume, it's easy to see the appeal of transforming myself into someone completely different—and I understand how trying on a new identity might embolden you to step beyond the established boundaries of your everyday personality. Even Bruce Wayne, despite all his money and power, vanquished crime effectively in Gotham only after donning his iconic Batman cape. Superhero garb, the psychologist and heroism expert Robin Rosenberg notes, can serve as a kind of effective visual shorthand, helping wearers feel reborn while simultaneously conveying their intended purpose to the outside world. "A costume of any sort is a signal both to the people who see it and the people who wear it. To the people who see it, it's an indication of what the person's role is. It makes real life superheroes feel stronger and more empowered."

But Franco questions some of the motivations behind real-life superheroes' missions. He thinks that, in some cases, the alternate identities they adopt may mask unresolved psychological issues. "It's often easier to resolve other people's problems than it is to try to resolve our own." He also suspects that some real-life superheroes may develop an addiction to the adrenaline rush that comes with interfering to stop a mugging, for example. "It's definitely a very exciting thing to be engaged in crime fighting. But I worry about people needing that sort of artificial high, not engaging with things that are more stable."

Another danger, Franco says, is that carrying out regular patrols with the express intent of performing heroic acts may tip the balance too far toward reckless intervention—if you attack a robber who's holding up a bank clerk, for instance, you could easily get killed your-self. "If you're in a situation that calls for heroism, it's a conundrum. Any step you take may be right or wrong in a big way. Being judicious in that situation is really key. The really heroic people are electing not to act in most situations, but in particular situations, they will act." In other words, prudent withdrawal—or alerting the person best quali-fied to deal with a particular situation—can be as much a part of effec-tive heroism as boldly inserting yourself into the fray. But Rosenberg points out that true selflessness often involves high-stakes choices that threaten personal safety. Some real-life superheroes, she says, "have made significant personal sacrifices to do what they do, which can be concerning. But that's true of anyone who makes significant sacrifices for other people."

Not only does the real-life superhero movement encourage inter-vention, it also broadens the traditional definition of a hero—weathering significant peril on behalf of a larger cause you believe in. While real-life superheroes may encounter danger at times, many of the things they typically do, like passing clothing out to the homeless, fall more under the heading of garden-variety altruism. But real-life superheroes are in no way solely responsible for giving the term "hero" a more inclusive definition than it once had. CNN's website, for instance, spotlights "CNN Heroes: Everyday People Changing the World," almost all of whom are remarkable altruists. The 2011 top 10 included Derreck Kayongo, the head of a nonprofit that supplies soap to poor communities, and Amy Stokes, who works to connect volun-teer mentors with South African children via the Internet. Few nomi-nees would be considered heroes in the traditional sense.

Real-life superheroes reject the notion that what they do dimin-ishes the extreme heroism of service members and death-defying rescuers. "It would be remiss for me to say that going to an animal shelter to drop off supplies is the same as going into battle," Prowler says, "[but] I think 'hero' can define people who are going above and beyond to make a difference. I'm not in boot camp and getting fired at, but I'm giving up my Saturdays to do this. I'm going a little above and beyond."

As Prowler sees it, there's a vast spectrum of different types of heroic action, and the existence of one shouldn't detract from the existence of another. She thinks any effort to improve someone else's situation is meaningful and commendable, whether you do it on the battlefield, in a Third World refugee camp, or in cat ears and tight leggings patrolling the streets of New York City. One upside of acknowledging highly altruistic acts as heroic, as Phil Zimbardo does and as real-life superheroes do, is that it makes heroism seem more accessible. Most of us find it hard to picture ourselves saving someone from a burning building or leading a protest march against the government; it's much easier to envision assembling care packages for the homeless or intervening in small neighborhood disputes before they lead to fights.

That's where the real-life superheroes' real value lies—in their democratization of the heroic ideal, in their insistence that it's attainable to anyone. It's a comfortably familiar, Protestant-work-ethic approach to heroism: If you put in the time and effort, you can consider yourself a hero. It's a more foolproof, more formulaic route than aiming for the outsized heroic acts championed in newspaper headlines, whose success depends much more heavily on niche expertise or random chance. If you're not a rescue worker by profession, there's little chance you're ever going to be able to save someone in the path of a tsunami or earthquake. But as long as you know people or animals are suffering out in the open, you can take concrete steps to relieve that suffering. It doesn't take being born with superpowers or winning the heroism lottery; it just takes dedication.

Now that Life and his co-heroes are beginning to attract more attention from the media and the outside world, heroism experts are watching with interest to see whether new membership will kick the real-life superhero movement into high gear or whether it will remain a fringe undertaking. Getting decked out in an elaborate costume on a regular basis is a decidedly out-of-the-ordinary activity, and it's only natural to wonder whether some recent recruits consider hero patrols an occasional weekend lark rather than a key part of their altruistic identity. "The more press it gets, the more people join it, the bigger it becomes. For those joiners, will it stick or is it a fad? Who knows," Rosenberg says. But she doesn't see the old-timers like Life and Shade as dilettantes; she believes they're unswervingly dedicated to their heroic goals. "The people that came to it before it got media attention—they did it because it was their passion. They want to make a difference, and if they inspire other people to make a difference, that's an added benefit."

After a self-defense workshop in the late afternoon, led by a couple of the more seasoned heroes, the Superheroes Anonymous conference begins to wind down. Some of the attendees leave, clad in their self-created capes and masks, as the sun begins to set. But for the most hardcore would-be heroes, there's one final event: Life's Homeless Outreach training workshop, to be followed by a group patrol session in the streets of Lower Manhattan.

We congregate at a couple of tables where the real-life superheroes have set out large boxes of donated items: travel shampoos and lotions, soaps, granola bars, mini Hershey bars, and rolled-up socks. We stuff an assortment of the loot into Ziplocs, filling them as full as we can before sealing them closed. On another table is a tangle of old clothes, things like oversized men's shirts, sweaters, and long-sleeved jerseys. After stuffing as many homeless outreach packs as we can into our totes and purses, we pile the clothing over our arms, as much as we

WHAT MAKES A HERO?

can carry. "We're going to go to a nearby drop-off point," Life announces, "keep our eyes and ears open, see if anyone needs help."

Life wends his way past an assortment of noodle houses and home-style Italian restaurants, leading the procession to a civic building on Leonard Street. There are already a few people outside, huddled against the cold, and when they see the piles of clothing in our arms, they approach us cautiously. Many seem to speak only Chinese, but once they understand why we're here, no common language seems necessary. The women appraise each item of clothing like they're at a swap meet, holding it at arm's length and scrutinizing it before deciding whether it belongs in their to-keep stack.

After all the onlookers have gotten what they need, we move on to a Christian mission just a few blocks away, where three men are smoking outside the doors. Life strikes up a conversation with one of them, who says he's originally from Georgia and wants to get his life back together here in New York. "God bless you," he says, shaking Life's hand. "Thank you for doing this work."

This kind of feedback—and the knowledge that they're helping real people in need—is what keeps Life and his band of heroic aspirants going. There's a decent number of people out there that see them as naïve to think they can make a difference, and another good-sized group who think they're just superficial attention-seekers. Nevertheless, they're convinced their actions are making things better. Their philosophy is a kind of pop-cultural take on the ancient Hebrew concept of *tikkun olam*, repairing the world, and their certainty in the value of their efforts goes a long way in helping them tune out their detractors.

Others may argue about the precise definition of heroism, the psychological significance of wearing costumes in public, and whether an intervention-first approach is prudent. It's all mostly background noise to the real-life superheroes themselves. Like Robin Hood's Merry

Men, they're most focused on helping the downtrodden and on passing the word along to anyone else who shares their vision and is willing to expend the effort to make it real. They know what they're doing isn't for everyone—wallflowers and cynics need not apply. But in transforming their heroic impulses into action, they're inspiring other would-be heroes and illustrating what happens when abstract ideals like compassion and altruism are unleashed in the gritty, churning laboratory of New York City. "There's a true altruistic spirit within everyone," Life tells the neophyte heroes at the meeting, who are clustered around him, absorbing his every word. "This is a chance to create it." In this moment, his optimism and drive feel utterly contagious. *If he can do it*, I think to myself, *why can't I?* Though I'll probably leave my tights and cape at home, planning a heroic venture of my own is starting to seem more and more appealing.

Chapter Eleven
TAKING THE HERO CHALLENGE

I f there's one thing I've learned, it's that heroes and extreme altruists are all around us—and that they're not necessarily the exalted figures we'd expect. Dave Hartsock enjoyed a burst of publicity after he rescued Shirley Dygert, but these days, he lives a quiet life, mostly undisturbed. Victoria Trabosh flies under the radar as founder of the Itafari Foundation, which supports aspiring Rwandan businesswomen. People who raise multiple needy foster kids or take care of lonely senior citizens might receive muted recognition within their local communities, but very few ascend to the heights of fame that reality TV stars achieve overnight.

All this reinforces a message I hear from heroism and altruism researchers: Heroes are mostly regular people who harness their desire to care for others and make an extraordinary commitment to reach out to them. Jeremy Frimer of the University of Winnipeg helped convince me when he described what he'd learned from surveying people who'd been given awards either for unusual one-shot bravery or for showing care for others over a longer period of time. By and large, members of the "bravery" group were completely ordinary in their personalities—the researchers didn't find many significant differences when they compared these gutsy award-winners to control subjects who had *not* received an award. "People that do these things are different in subtle ways," Frimer says. And while members of the "caring" group scored higher than average in nurturance and other similar traits, a so-called prosocial personality is far from the sole determinant of whether people are likely to carry out selfless acts— more than one personality type leads to such behavior.

But as Frimer notes, altruistic whizzes do tend to make some important choices in their approach to life. Like Jodee Blanco and Ervin Staub, heroes have a tendency to see what happens to them through a redemptive lens. "You can talk about a tragedy and they'll say something good came out of it," he says. "They might see the suffering as an opportunity to find meaning and purpose in their lives." And like Allan Luks and Mike Hrostoski, they firmly believe that their own well-being is aligned with the well-being of people around them— that life is not a zero-sum game where succeeding necessarily means triumphing over others. In the stories morally motivated heroes tell about their lives, Frimer says, "they pull together themes of power and achievement with themes of communion. It's like they don't want one to happen without the other." Similarly, when the UC Irvine political scientist Kristen Monroe compared a group of World War II heroic rescuers to a group of bystanders, she found that what set the rescuers apart was the way they looked at the world. Not only did they view themselves as more capable of getting things done, but they tended to view themselves as part of the vast human family rather than as members of more exclusive groups.

Findings like these are empowering, reflecting what Zimbardo, Doty, and other altruism luminaries claim: that we have the potential to transform ourselves into heroes and altruists if we approach the task the right way. At the same time, it's got me thinking more and more about my own heroic obligations. If what the researchers say is true—that I'm fully capable of following in the heroic footsteps of people like Dave Hartsock and Jodee Blanco—what excuse do I have to hang back? Don't I owe it to the world to try?

If I want to take a shot at strengthening my heroic capabilities, though, I need to be realistic. I know full-fledged traditional physical heroism is a long shot for someone like me. I'm not likely to encounter a situation where someone nearby is in dire peril. I'm also about the furthest thing from Xena there is—in high school gym class, I struggled to do just a handful of pull-ups, and I can't deal with the thought of putting my life on the line three times a week or more, like soldiers or volunteer firefighters do. So even if a chance opportunity for physical heroism ever arises, I probably won't be equipped to seize it. (There's almost certainly a degree of truth to that assumption: A study of thirty-two "physical heroes" who stepped in to help robbery and assault victims found that split-second white knights were physically larger and more likely to have completed rescue training than members of a control group who'd never intervened.)

My study of selflessness, though, has inspired me to start thinking about heroism in a much broader sense. You don't have to be an adrenaline junkie or in tip-top physical shape to dedicate your life to a cause larger than yourself, or have to sacrifice something huge to stand up for what you believe in. Working to make life better for others is something I feel confident I can do.

Anticipating that most other aspiring heroes don't envision turning themselves into Superman or Wonder Woman clones, Zimbardo geared his Heroic Imagination Project largely toward creating "everyday heroes" such as potential moral whistle-blowers and people who aren't afraid to help others in the vicinity. A big part of becoming a hero in the real world, he believes, involves training yourself to resist known psychological influences that will hold you back from intervening in situations—big or small—where you have a real chance to help others or stop injustice. He put together a series of online videos to supply would-be heroes with the skills they'll need to recognize and resist these influences. I decide to take in some of these videos with the idea that they might help equip me for future heroic intervention. The videos won't be the same as a hero boot camp (as far as I know, no such thing currently exists for adults), but I'm hoping they'll serve as a kind of virtual crash course.

One of the first videos I watch is about the infamous Milgram experiments and what they reveal about people's frightening willingness to submit to authority. The video highlights something I never realized: Some experimental subjects instructed to "shock" other participants showed clear signs of conflict, especially when they heard the participants' screams and cries of pain from the room next door. They paused as if dreading the thought of continuing their electrical assault; only when the experiment leader told them they had to continue would they resume the shocks. One "teacher" muttered, "I can't stand it." In the end, though, about two-thirds of the teachers moved all the way up the shock continuum, from "strong" to "very strong" to "severe"— 450 volts. "In a new situation, those social factors in that context can sway us in ways we don't realize," Zimbardo warns at the end of the video.

I'd like to believe I would have been one of the rare dissenters, ready to defy the experimenter, but I know there can be a massive difference between what you *think* you'll do if you find yourself in a Milgram-style situation and what you *actually* do. I resolve to speak up early and loudly if some authority gives me an order I'm not comfortable with or if I see some socially sanctioned injustice taking place, but I know only time will prove whether I'll have the confidence and presence of mind I need in the pressure of the moment.

Another video recounts the cautionary tale of the doomed college fraternity initiate Matthew Carrington. In order to earn membership, Carrington had to participate in the time-tested rite of hazing, which can involve wearing miniskirts while standing at a busy intersection, trading clothes with a homeless person, and more. All pretty harmless stuff—until things started to escalate on the third night of "Hell Week." The pledges were ordered to hold a five-gallon water jug weighing 42 pounds, stand on one foot, and drink as much of the water as they could. After drinking a large amount of water, Carrington started acting confused and disoriented. Another fraternity member walked in, drunk, and ordered him to perform push-ups. It wasn't long before he reached a point of no return. "He just all of a sudden dropped," J. P. Fickes, one of the witnesses, said, "and it seemed like his whole body just tensed up." Starting to realize something was wrong, Fickes got out his cell phone and typed 911 into the number field. But one of the other members said, "It's OK, you don't need to call 911—Matt's just sleeping." As a result, Fickes hit the red button on his phone, to cancel the call, instead of the green button, to make the call. In short, he failed to do what was needed to help Carrington because those around him were telling him, through their words and actions, that it was all right not to.

As I'm watching, I think about how I once lived in a neighborhood in San Francisco that was only a few blocks from the Tenderloin—the nexus of the city's drug dealing and prostitution, and ground zero for many of its homeless. Uncomfortably, I remember that if I happened to see someone lying on the sidewalk, seemingly near death, I was much more likely to hurry past, along with everyone else, than attempt to do anything to help them. I'd lived in the city long enough that I'd become desensitized to such sights, and even when the person's distress penetrated my brain deeply enough to bother me, it was easy to quicken my pace when I saw a dozen people in front of me doing the same thing. I decide that instead of walking faster the next time I see someone struggling, I'm going to slow down, take the time to process what's in front of me, and make a fully conscious decision about whether to help.

In addition to warning against the dangers of conformity and inaction, Zimbardo encourages would-be heroes to flex their altruistic muscles by taking a specific action that will make a small change in the world. This directive seems too simplistic at first—theoretically, recycling my paper and cans makes a change in the world, and I don't feel like doing so is heroic in the least. Still, I figure, I can make some small difference in people's lives, even if it doesn't make a dent in world hunger or redress major social injustices. I remember the guiding principle of Lynne Henderson's social-fitness regimen: In order to take a risky action that's out of the ordinary, you need to start small and build your confidence so you'll be comfortable repeating similar actions later on.

I think a lot about what I want my change-creating action to be. I could do a one-day fund-raiser for a cause close to my heart. I could ask people to donate to a worthy cause on my birthday instead of giving me gifts. But I want to do something that feels a little more meaningful—something that allows me to get more directly involved in the change-creation process, maybe even something that scares me a little. I think of the real-life superheroes I met in New York City, the ones who went on patrols to help relieve other people's suffering, even though they knew their actions made only a small dent in overwhelming social problems. In the past, I've shied away from one-on-one altruistic action because problems like homelessness and poverty *do* seem so large, so insurmountable, but talking with the real-life superheroes has made it clear that they focus on the situations they *are* able to improve rather than on the magnitude of the problems they can't control.

I think uncomfortably of the Matthew Carrington video, the way it reminded me of how I'd passed by so many people right in front of me who were obviously hurting. I want to try to make amends for that habitual oversight. Out of the blue, I remember something my middle school English teacher, Kate Sussman, wrote on one of my class papers: "Look at every human being you meet as unique and particular." That's what Life was doing the night we delivered "care packages" to homeless New York City residents: not just giving them things they needed, like toothpaste, socks, and washcloths, but actually getting to know them, interacting with them like fellow human beings instead of untouchables. I decide that's what I want to attempt, but this time, on my own.

Remembering that Life mentioned that many homeless people have plenty of food—what many really need are other necessities—I raid my own toiletry closet for leftover freebies and dentist's-office samples. Then I head to the Dollar Tree website and order a whole pile of stuff: bulk toothbrushes, washcloths, mini tubes of toothpaste. Each of the care packages I assemble in Ziploc freezer bags includes a bar of soap, a washcloth, a toothbrush, a small tube of toothpaste, a comb, and a small container of breadsticks and cheese, the same pre-packaged kind I used to eat as a kid. What I'm putting together reminds me of the kits the airlines give you when you're stranded overnight after a missed flight. But while those travelers get put up in a complimentary hotel and return to their regular lives the next morning, the people I'll be meeting are in the midst of a limbo with no defined beginning and end.

I'm a little apprehensive the morning of my trip to San Francisco. I'm thirty weeks pregnant, and I'm not sure how people are going to react to me. Will I be safe? Will anyone try to jump me? I tell myself not to worry; after all, I lived in the city for more than two years, just blocks from where I'm going to be carrying out my mission, and no one ever gave me any serious trouble. I wish I could head into this adventure with no fear, but my type-A personality (and my pregnant belly) won't allow it.

As soon as I step off the Caltrain, I spot a wheeled cart in the station lobby with a green sleeping bag wadded into its base and a half-empty two-liter Pepsi on top. I figure there must be an itinerant owner nearby, and sure enough, I spot a tall man with greasy gray hair standing just outside the lobby, chain-smoking and pacing back and forth in the rising sun. I approach him and ask if he wants a care package, describing some of the contents to him—toothpaste, soap, a washcloth. He shakes his head, bored. "No, thanks."

"OK." I turn to go, but before I can take more than a couple steps, he says, "A lot of people, they wouldn't take that even if you tried to give it to them."

"How come?" I say.

He raises his eyebrows. "Just look at how they live. They're not gonna use it." I'm struck by his use of *they* instead of *we*. Suddenly, I wonder if he's standing twenty feet away from his cart so people won't realize it belongs to him.

"Are you sure you don't want one?" I say, holding the bag out to him again. He reaches for it. "All right," he says, "I'll give it to someone else." This initial encounter leaves me wondering what other kinds of reactions I'm going to get. I haven't pictured being turned down by people who obviously need help, but my station acquaintance's words alert me to the possibility. Of course, I remind myself, no one should have to take something they don't want.

I hop on the Muni train from the Caltrain station to the Powell Street cable-car turnaround, just blocks from where I once lived in San Francisco. This intersection is one of the city's biggest tourist hotspots—the line for a cable-car ride stretches nearly all the way to the corner of the next block—but it's also a big gathering spot for homeless residents. As I step out of the underground Muni station into the sun, I see an older black man in a wheelchair perched at the top of a flight of stairs leading to the street. There's a copy of *Street Sheet* in his lap, a publication the city's homeless sometimes sell instead of panhandling, but he doesn't appear to be making any particular effort to interest passersby in the paper; it sits limp and ignored in his lap. When I offer him a care package, his head rises from his chest just a little. "Thank you, I can use that," he mumbles, not looking at me.

I chat with a few more people as I make my way up Powell Street toward Union Square. One—a tiny woman with eyes as green as a jungle cat's—takes the bag, but makes it clear that what she really wants is money. I dig through my wallet and scrounge up seventy-five cents. Just ahead, there's a trifecta on the corner of Powell and O'Farrell: a wheelchair-bound woman with aqua-blue hair sifting through a plastic box filled with rose petals, a dog curled up at her feet; a skinny black man in a Western hat; and a youngish-looking white guy with a dark brown beard. The man in the hat thanks me profusely, and when I glance backward on my way across the street, I see him tucking into his package of breadsticks with gusto.

When I hand a care package to the bearded guy, who's sitting on the side of the street I've just crossed to, he says, "Thank you very much." I kneel so I can look into his face. "How are you feeling?" he says—a question I get a lot these days, now that my pregnancy is obvious.

Pretty good, I say, just getting around a little more slowly than usual. "How long have you been living in the city?" I ask.

"I've been spazzin' around here since '94." He tells me how he's going to start looking for a job soon, just something entry-level. "Paperwork and filing, maybe. Baby steps." We chat for a few more minutes, and he sees me off with a luminous smile.

Once I pass the O'Farrell intersection, I make my way to Union Square proper—a large, open concrete plaza flanked here and there with strips of grass. I sit down on one of the benches in the middle of the square and start scribbling in my notepad. After a few moments, a man toting a bouquet of brightly colored helium balloons sits down next to me. "What you got in that notebook?" he says. I explain that I am a writer. "I need help," he says, as a preamble, then strikes up a conversation. "Where you from?"

When I say San Jose, he nods knowingly. "That used to be a good place to visit when I was there in the seventies." He's brimming with flattery, telling me I remind him of Sally Field. I tell him I can't use a balloon, but that I do have toiletry kits in my suitcase if he's interested. When I pull one out to show him, though, his demeanor completely changes. "Oh, you're giving things to the *homeless*," he says, his voice dripping with sarcasm. "I bet that makes you feel real smart."

I protest, but he's not having any of it. "You're writing about them, but you don't know anything about their lives. Now, how's that make you feel when I say it? I bet it makes you feel real dumb. Fuck you, you skinny-ass white bitch." Shaken, I get up, grab the suitcase handle, and start walking away as fast as I can.

I tell myself the guy is crazy, but the encounter still smarts, because I recognize a kernel of truth in what he's saying. From his perspective, here's a fairly well-off looking white girl condescending to give him something so she can feel good about herself, then flouncing back to her privileged life, never to be heard from again. (And in a way, he's right—I'll never be able to understand exactly what people living on the streets are going through on a daily basis, much as I'd like to.) His insinuation that I'm exploiting people by writing about my experience hurts, too.

After heading out of Union Square, I take a left and head down Mason toward Market Street. I offer care packages to a couple people sitting on street corners, but they're not interested—one woman tells me she just wants two things, a hamburger and a fresh needle, so I have to move on. Just as I approach Market, I notice what looks like a small cart traveling down the sidewalk, but, on closer inspection, it's actually a wheelchair piled high with miscellaneous items. I greet the woman pushing the chair, who introduces herself as Gail, and ask her if she wants a care package. "You got anything else?" she says as I hand her the package—meaning money, I assume. I shake my head, but offer her another care package, and she sets it on the top of the pile of belongings in her wheelchair.

I ask her how she got here, and she tells me she came to San Francisco about a year ago to be closer to her daughter. "She's homeless, I'm homeless." Things haven't been easy for her since then, she says. "I have diabetes, and it's hard for me to get around." She explains that the reason she's not sitting in her wheelchair is that it's gotten too small for her, and she hasn't yet been able to secure a larger one from the agencies that donate them.

Still, Gail seems to be holding on to hope. She pulls a bright yellow flier, which looks to be from a local housing authority, out of the pile in her wheelchair. "This lady told me to call her around two, and I might be able to get into this place." Many homeless people, I know, dream of getting off the streets into someplace safe and dry—someplace with a mailing address where they can receive welfare checks, which may help keep them afloat until they apply for a job. "I hope things get better for you and your daughter," I say, squeezing Gail's hand. The words feel futile as soon as they leave my mouth, but I'm not sure what else to say or do.

After a short lunch break, I calculate I still have about half of my care packages left, so I decide to head over to the Civic Center Muni stop just outside City Hall. As soon as I step off the train into the station, I spot a large black man sitting on one of the commuter benches, surrounded by plastic garbage bags. I show him a care package and ask if he'd like one, and his face breaks into a huge, infectious grin. "This is exactly what I needed!" he exclaims. He introduces himself as Walter, and he seems especially excited about the tube of Aquafresh toothpaste in the bag. "I just ran out of toothpaste, and they didn't have any at the shelter. Then they got some, but it was the generic kind. This stuff is better."

He asks me about what I'm up to, and I explain my project to him. He listens, interested. "Some people probably don't appreciate what you're doing, right?" he says. I nod and tell him about getting cursed out at Union Square earlier. "You're getting led the right way," he reassures me as I get ready to head outside. "In forty-eight years, I have never gone out and done something nice for someone else like that. You make me want to."

From my days living in the city, I remember that homeless people often congregate near Civic Center, but the sight that greets me as I emerge from the station still takes me by surprise. Two grassy strips flank a wide expanse of concrete—a pedestrian thoroughfare most of the city's nonhomeless residents steer clear of. Sitting, standing, lounging, lolling on either side of the walkway are dozens of homeless people lined up all the way to the corner. Some are zoned out, apparently dead to the world, while others are chatting animatedly to themselves or one another. It's a scene straight out of the Third World. While other U.S. cities—New York, for instance—have made concerted efforts to sweep their homeless residents out of sight, they're out in the open here. I don't see cops anywhere; maybe they prefer to stay away.

I approach a man in a wheelchair who says his name's Donovan. He thanks me for the care package and we talk a little about our lives and my upcoming baby. Seeing what I've got in my suitcase, a few other people stroll up to me, asking, "You got any more of those?" I reach into my suitcase and hand out the care packages as fast as I can, hoping there will be enough for everyone who wants one and trying to make eye contact with each recipient. Once all of the requesters have gotten a package, I walk over to a concrete ledge where a few more people are sitting. As I'm handing one man a baggie, he asks me, "How far along are you?" When I tell him, he breaks into a smile and tells me his girlfriend is also thirty weeks pregnant. "It's a little girl," he says, smiling. We wish each other well for the life-changing weeks ahead.

By 2:30 in the afternoon—less than half an hour after my arrival at Civic Center—my care packages are completely gone. I wish I had another thirty to give away; there are more than enough potential recipients within a thousand-foot radius. But I don't, so I say good-bye to the people I've met and head back to the Civic Center subway station, my rolling suitcase now so lightweight it bounces and skips off the concrete.

Do acts of goodwill like my San Francisco trip actually enhance our ability to step up, should we ever face the kind of heroic choice that involves a high level of personal sacrifice? When I get a chance to ask Zimbardo the big question point-blank, he says he's found that people who report giving time to others on a regular basis are also more likely to report sacrificing themselves in a significant way for someone else. "There's a high correlation between volunteering significantly, sixty hours a year, and doing a heroic deed."

This correlation, of course, does not necessarily imply a causative relationship; the possible connections between altruism and subsequent heroism still need to be studied more extensively. But if consistently performing helpful or kind acts *does* sharpen our heroic capabilities, what mechanism may be at work? Zimbardo points out that selfless acts give us concrete practice at being prosocially oriented—that is, being aware of and attuned to other people's needs and desires. "If you're not sociocentric," he says, "you're never going to be a hero because you'll never notice someone is in need." That's why he sees volunteering, complimenting other people, and other low-key socially oriented ventures as good training for heroic action. Such acts force us to set our egos aside at least temporarily in order to focus on others. As a bonus, the more often we practice these kinds of prosocial acts, the more often we typically *want* to practice them, since we're likely to want to recapture the positive feelings we get from extending ourselves for others. Generally, the more hours people spend volunteering, the more likely they are to continue volunteering in the future.

On the other hand, giving experiments like mine, even when repeated on a regular basis, do not necessarily a well-rounded hero make. Regardless of how many times you prepare food for the homeless or volunteer to teach young children to read, you might not feel adequately equipped to, say, fish a drowning person out of an icy lake. The psychologist Robin Rosenberg points out that that one kind of heroic "trial run" won't necessarily prepare you for a different type of real-life scenario. "Giving up your seat [on the bus] is great, but I'm not sure if it would make someone more likely to intervene if they see someone being mugged."

Zimbardo maintains that prosocially oriented practice is a key ingredient of preparing yourself for heroic action, but he says it's not the whole story. He believes "situational awareness"—the ability to accurately assess just what a given situation requires—is another key element of heroic priming. Informing yourself about common psychological pitfalls is an ideal way to develop this kind of awareness, he says, which is why HIP educational programs contain such a hefty helping of psychological case studies like the Milgram experiments. The awareness you acquire from learning about forces that could potentially nudge you into inaction, he says, "gives you a special kind of knowledge. In HIP, we make explicit, 'Now that you've got knowledge, you've got to act.'"

Once you know about the general human propensity to go along with the crowd even when the crowd's judgment is nonsensical or immoral, Zimbardo's thinking goes, you're better equipped to help a woman who's coughing uncontrollably in the middle of the sidewalk, even when no one else is breaking their stride to see what's wrong. And once you're able to read a social situation at work in a matter of seconds and realize that your colleagues are caving in to a superior's immoral request, the way the subjects in the Milgram experiments did, you've got the ammunition you need to either entreat your colleagues to stop or relay your concerns to a superior who can effectively address the problem. Without that background knowledge, you might not be able to muster the motivation you need to step forward.

Zimbardo likes to tell a story about a high school student named Phillip who completed one of HIP's educational programs. Riding on a bus one day, he noticed that one of the other riders appeared to be having a severe asthma attack. No one else made a move to help the rider, but Phillip saw an opportunity to act. He asked the rider, "What's wrong?" Once he got a clear explanation, he directed the driver to stop the bus immediately and ran to get the rider some help. Though no large-scale studies exist to date on the connection between situational awareness training and subsequent heroic action, Zimbardo sees Phillip's story as a compelling illustration of how such training can make us more likely to intervene to help others when necessary. "When he was asked, 'Why did you do this?' he said, 'I knew it was the bystander effect in action. I learned at HIP that I had to take action, and I did.'"

Developing situational awareness means cultivating the ability to size up a real-world situation and determining what you can do to help—which also involves realizing that the wisest course of action may not include getting directly involved. So if you see someone being mugged but don't feel physically prepared to fend off an attacker, you might be better off yelling at the top of your lungs and pointing, or calling 911 on your cell phone to bring cops to the scene. "You have to know how to do it right. Step back, size it up," Zimbardo says. "What is happening here? What needs to be resolved? What can I do alone, and what can I do with others? Do I need to do something else to get help?" If you envision yourself as a more traditional physical hero, it certainly can't hurt to get training in areas like CPR and self-defense to ready yourself for potential rescues. But it's comforting to me, since I can't see myself fitting the macho mold, to realize that heroic action can arise as surely from shrewd judgment as from physical brawn. Sometimes that kind of considered judgment requires would-be heroes to take their egos out of the situation. Running into the fray to try to stop a crime might earn you recognition for your bravery, but it might also land you on the obituaries page—a tragedy, considering that alerting nearby authorities might have resolved the crime just as effectively.

As I ride the train back toward Montgomery station after my self-imposed hero training mission, my suitcase now empty of care packages, I think about whether I'd do something like this again. Probably, I decide, although I'd be more likely to do it with someone else. The Union Square balloon seller's tirade was a sobering reminder that this kind of mission isn't without its risks, so a strength-in-numbers strategy seems more sensible. I know there are plenty of people out there who are likely to look askance at ventures like this, pegging me as someone looking to shore up her own self-worth by giving stuff away. But even though the day included some scary and depressing moments, there were more than enough moments of positivity and genuine connection to make up for them.

More than passing out the care packages, though, what sustained me and motivated me to do this again was the level of near-instant rapport I was able to develop with the people I spoke to, many of whom were used to being ignored. It was the most surprising occurrence of the day, one that at times seemed miraculous. Offered a meager gift and a little kindness, people the world had written off as hopeless opened up the way parched blooms do after a few drops of rain. This experience has encouraged me to seek out small but essential moments of connection with strangers on a daily basis, even if I don't have any care packages to give away. A smile or a genuinely supportive word, as my friend Jill Neimark points out, can be just as meaningful as a snack or a tube of toothpaste, maybe more so. Similarly, this venture reminds me that in my mentoring work with kids, my company and steadfast support are more important than anything else I can provide.

Staring out the train window, I also think about how easily and how profoundly helping missions like mine can fall short. Our intentions may be good when we approach people with an offer of aid, but how they react—and how far our gestures ultimately go in improving the situation—is usually out of our control. People may take offense and reject help outright, as the Union Square balloon seller did. They may fail to acknowledge a condolence card or a visit. They may assume we will ultimately want something from them in return. Despite all this—despite the myriad ways a gesture of goodwill can get lost in translation—what choice do we have? Either we approach people with our meager offerings, fully and uncomfortably conscious that these offerings cannot always mend what is broken, or we hang back, content to allow pain or injustice to persist. Action seems by far the better response, despite the very real risk of offending, of falling short, of being brushed aside. At the same time, we need to proceed with caution and humility, to address the people we're trying to help as equals and human beings, not "targets" in need of aid.

Going into my giving experiment, I was skeptical, but now—thanks to the encouragement I've received from the people I helped—I understand better how low-key ventures like this fit into my larger quest for selflessness. Educating ourselves about what's truly needed in a given situation, becoming aware of common pitfalls that might prevent us from helping, and pushing ourselves to carry out generous acts on a regular basis: All of these measures revise our outlook in a fundamental way. Where before heroic opportunities passed by like Shakespeare's "insubstantial pageant" or like shadows on a cave wall, they begin to come into sharp focus and reveal themselves in full color. It's precisely that clear-seeing capability that inspires us to turn our altruistic impulses into real-world action.

Chapter Twelve
CULTIVATING A HEROIC LIFE

n the year 2002, Christoph von Toggenburg embarked on an audacious journey: biking all the way from India to Switzerland to raise money for leprosy victims, a distance of more than six thousand miles. Not only would he have to bike dozens of miles per day in order to keep the pace, he would have to bike through some of the poorest and most politically unstable regions on the planet, including parts of Iran and Pakistan. Some days were so difficult that he wasn't sure whether he could keep going. When sandstorms kicked up, as they often do in the desert, the howling winds felt like a slap in the face. Sweat dripped down his body as he pedaled under a scorching sun in temperatures that sometimes topped 100 degrees Fahrenheit.

As von Toggenburg proceeded on his journey, he wrote long newsletters about his experiences that he sent to members of e-mail lists, and people began to tune in regularly to read his updates. In the end, von Toggenburg was able to raise about $500,000 for his cause, but he also ascended into the role of unofficial ambassador for the plight of leprosy victims worldwide. "Leprosy is a disgusting disease.

It was really giving a voice to those who don't have a voice," he says in a lilting Swiss accent. "It was very nice for me to be able to provide that."

To the rest of the world, von Toggenburg's bike ride might have seemed like an extraordinary act. But it was actually an act in keeping with the unique life he has built, one dedicated in a dizzying variety of ways to improving others' lot. Raised in two small villages set high in the Swiss Alps, von Toggenburg came from a family that traditionally belonged to the nobility—his ancestors controlled parts of Switzerland hundreds of years ago. But he always knew he didn't want to go through life coasting on his name or his inheritance. His mother and father were both doctors, so he grew up seeing helping others more as a responsibility than as an unusual act. Starting when he was six years old, his parents encouraged him to spend time with the elderly and disabled, which helped him to become comfortable with people who looked and acted different from the norm. By college, he was working closely with the homeless, and in the late 1990s, he launched his first major fund-raising project, Run for Help, running nearly 170 miles through the Alps in four and a half days and donating all of the proceeds to homeless kids in Romania. The success of that venture inspired him to create Bike for Help. "The basic philosophy was just that one can make a difference for many," he says. "If you as an individual stand up and use all your energies to make things move, you can make life better for others."

After finishing his epic bike ride, von Toggenburg decided to work for the International Committee of the Red Cross (ICRC)—a position that often placed him directly in harm's way. He was stationed in a series of global hot spots, including Nepal, Colombia, and the occupied Palestinian territories. In 2006, he and his colleagues were ambushed by unknown armed men in the Central African Republic; bullets pierced the outside of their Jeep as they revved to get away. "We only escaped by luck," he says. But being so close to suffering had unexpected fringe benefits: It helped him appreciate the opportunities in his own life and strengthened his conviction that he needs to use his time wisely. "It's a philosophy that I live—the idea of *carpe diem*. Any of us can just walk out the front door and die, and I mean this in the most positive sense. Because the whole system is so fragile, I like to live to the fullest."

Von Toggenburg's long-distance fund-raisers and his ICRC stint also had another crucial upside: They showed him just how effectively he could help others, provided he was willing to devote the time and effort. As long as he *could* help—as long as he was in a logistical and financial position to do so—how could he not? How could he turn away from the plight of lepers or unarmed civilians in a war zone, knowing exactly what was going to happen to them if he did?

Despite the accolades he's received, von Toggenburg is humble about what he's managed to achieve. Many people, he says, have asked him where he finds the stamina to get involved in so many demanding projects. The answer is simple: He genuinely enjoys what he does and it makes him feel useful, so he wants to keep doing more of it. "You see the effect it has, and that's a strong motivator. It's important to do that first step and feel, 'Wow, it's a nice thing. I want to do it again.'"

We admire heroes and extreme altruists not because we hope to emulate every single aspect of their lives, but because their courage inspires us. People like Christoph von Toggenburg are living metaphors, symbols of what many of us dream we could someday attain. They become central characters in the challenges we pose to ourselves: not *What would these people do?* so much as *What would they do if they found themselves in my situation?* But whether such thought experiments are actually productive is another matter. Can we actually distill the essence of the altruists and heroes we look up to, internalize their best attributes, and use those qualities to tackle the challenging situations we encounter in our own lives? In short, can we will ourselves to become what Phil Zimbardo calls everyday heroes?

While science has supplied some optimistic answers so far, it offers no easy shortcuts. The preponderance of evidence indicates that heroes are made rather than simply born. Developing heroic qualities like empathy, courage, altruism, and compassion is possible through deliberate practice, much as it's possible to learn to play a sonata in a month by practicing piano thirty minutes a day. Generally, becoming more altruistic isn't an overnight transformation; it's a steady climb. Christoph von Toggenburg worked with the elderly and homeless for years before launching the fund-raising ventures that transformed the lives of thousands and propelled him to worldwide acclaim. Dave Hartsock completed countless dives as an instructor and grew steeped in the moral code that governs the skydiving world before he embarked on the fateful dive where he saved Shirley Dygert's life. We often make the mistake of assuming we either do or do not possess heroic or altruistic traits ("I'm just not a people person" or "I could never sacrifice my life for someone else") without considering that such traits can grow much stronger with the right encouragement. "Fifty percent is genetic and ten percent environmental, but forty percent is choices and practices the individual pursues," Berkeley's Dacher Keltner says. "Out of the gate, we can change a lot."

But such heroic qualities don't just emerge at a moment's notice. I know all too well that it's easy enough to latch on to the idea of "becoming a hero," drop in at a meeting of real-life superheroes, or sign up for a weekend training course to become a volunteer firefighter. It's a lot harder to make the pursuit of heroism and altruism a long-term, deeply ingrained part of your lifestyle. This long-term investment, though, is the key to dramatic, sustained personal change—and it helps answer the essential question Shirley Dygert asked after Dave

Hartsock saved her life: "How can somebody have that much love for another person?" More than anything, cultivating the kind of great love that inspires true heroism requires careful and sustained preparation. We might be born with certain predispositions (to listen to our friends when they're talking about their problems, or, conversely, to tune them out and flip on ESPN), but we can refine capabilities like listening, generating empathy, and taking compassionate action by practicing them over and over again. As Lynne Henderson is demonstrating through her corporate ethics initiative, people can be trained to take a moral stand in the workplace or at school through targeted rehearsal—a specialized form of practice.

Of course, exerting this kind of sustained effort on behalf of others requires a substantial capacity to delay the gratification of your own needs, which is the trickiest part. "Self-control partly evolved to enable us to do altruistic things," says Roy Baumeister, a psychologist at Florida State University and author of *Willpower: Rediscovering the Greatest Human Strength*. Being selfish, he adds, is many people's natural pattern—it takes some degree of willpower to overcome it and ascend into the realm of altruism or heroism. He found that people who score high on measures of self-control tend to be more helpful and generous toward others than people whose reserves of self-control are depleted.

Baumeister's research suggests that strengthening your overall self-discipline may pay dividends in increasing your capacity to empathize with and show compassion for others. "Willpower is one resource you use for everything," Baumeister says. "You strengthen it for one thing and you're good to go for everything else." That means, for example, that if you start a twice-weekly exercise program and manage to make yourself stick with it for some time, you'll probably also be more likely to stick to altruism-related goals, such as carrying out planned volunteering projects or reaching out to people in need.

"Altruism and heroism take willpower, but you can strengthen the muscle."

This kind of mental strength training might sound intimidating, but the good news is that the longer you do it, the easier it gets. When we learn how to focus our attention, repeatedly doing things that are important to us, these new habits become hard-wired into our brains, making it easier and easier to carry them out—and even making us feel uncomfortable when we're *not* doing so. When we carry out the same altruistic behaviors day after day or week after week, then— whether it's mentoring kids, serving food at a soup kitchen, or asking others if they need help—our brains will gradually rewire themselves to reflect the reality we have chosen.

While willpower and repetition are essential components of shaping a heroic persona, that principle comes with a caveat. Baumeister has also found that willpower is a finite quantity that can get temporarily tapped out, meaning that if we devote large amounts of willpower to specific daily tasks, such as eating a Spartan meal for lunch, we may not have as much left in the tank immediately after to follow through on other tasks that require willpower, like keeping volunteer commitments or reaching out to someone in need. (This temporary depletion effect doesn't change the fact that strengthening your self-discipline *over time* can increase your altruistic capacities in the long run.)

To help make sure your altruistic tank isn't regularly hitting empty, it makes sense to choose altruistic commitments that you enjoy for their own sake. If you're volunteering somewhere only because it makes you feel virtuous afterward or because you feel like you "should" be doing it, the effort may take an outsized toll on your willpower reserves. To balance your altruistic goals with the rest of your life, throw yourself into ventures that really matter to you; if you're not enjoying yourself while you're helping, something's wrong with your approach. If you're passionate about giving children a chance to live a better life, for example, sign up to volunteer with an organization that allows you to mentor underprivileged kids. If your altruistic efforts aren't closely aligned with your most fundamental goals, they're more likely to fizzle out over time.

This is where Christoph von Toggenburg's remarkable altruistic trajectory is instructive to people hoping to follow in his footsteps. He readily admits that he does what he does in part because he enjoys it. "We look at altruism like you either do something for yourself *or* you do it for others. But it's a combination. I like sports, but I combine my passion with helping people. There is a feel-good factor where you can say, 'Wow, I've done that. It was difficult, but it was fun.'" How he describes feeling is exactly how I feel when I manage to get myself out of bed early to mentor at-risk high school kids in San Jose or distribute care packages to San Francisco's street residents. As Allan Luks might have predicted, I'm helping strengthen them, but I'm strengthening myself at the same time.

In addition to building up your willpower and knowing what causes truly fire you up, you also need to get yourself in the right frame of mind to step into a heroic or altruistic identity. Phillip Shaver, a psychologist at the University of California, Davis, has found that when people feel more secure in their relationships, they are more likely to be helpful to others. Similarly, it pays to surround yourself with role models who embody the characteristics of empathy and generosity that you'd like to achieve. When Samuel Oliner, himself a Holocaust survivor, conducted extensive interviews with Holocaust rescuers, he found that they tended to form close relationships and had a strong sense of responsibility for the welfare of others—characteristics would-be heroes would do well to emulate. Many of the heroic rescuers in Oliner's studies reported that family members had shown them the importance of caring for others over long periods of time, which may have helped prepare them for the demands of heroic intervention.

Your own role model "family" doesn't have to be blood relations, of course; they just have to have altruistic goals similar to your own and a track record of achieving them. Like Life and other real-life superheroes, you can assemble your own impromptu tribe of kindred spirits who push you to behave more selflessly and more heroically. In cheering one another's efforts, you'll help ensure that none of you fall off the altruistic wagon.

To increase the likelihood that you'll feel empathy for other people, it also helps to think specifically about what you have in common with them. "When I think about how people can be altruistic or kind, I think about the notion of establishing a common group identity," says the University of California, Berkeley, psychologist Rudy Mendoza-Denton. "Sports fans who have no relation to each other— other than that they like the same sports team—will hug each other, be kind to each other, and feel a certain unity. Similarly, New York is always such a difficult town, but in the wake of 9/11 there was this huge identity around the idea of being New Yorkers. All the intergroup walls really fell."

The more broadly you define the "groups" you belong to, the more likely you are to feel compassion for a larger number of people and feel predisposed to help them. The Northeastern University psychologist David DeSteno and his colleagues told experimental subjects they were doing a study on musical perception, then had them tap their hands in time to a beat. While they were doing so, they could see another "participant"—actually a confederate of the researchers— who was also tapping, either in time with them or randomly. Soon afterward, the subjects watched as yet another confederate cheated this fellow "participant" by assigning him to a long, onerous task without using a computerized randomizer to establish whether he should get stuck with the task or not. DeSteno found that the subjects who'd been tapping their hands in unison with the other "participant" felt more compassion for him when he was cheated and were also likely to spend more time helping him out when he was unfairly assigned to the long task.

These results bolster Mendoza-Denton's view that establishing a common identity with others goes a long way toward increasing the likelihood that we'll be moved to help when they're in need. "We can cultivate compassion effortlessly from the bottom up," DeSteno told attendees at Telluride's Science of Compassion conference, "by changing the way we think about other people. Think about your neighbor as the person who likes Starbucks as much as you do. What we're arguing for is to emphasize the similarities between people." That may also mean building rapport with members of unfamiliar groups by striving to get to know them as unique and particular individuals, a tactic Paul Slovic's research suggests will greatly increase our willingness to help them. When you meet a homeless man on the streets of San Francisco or see the face of a Rwandan boy in the newspaper, think of him not as an "other" or a "foreigner," but as someone who's suffered disappointment and deprivation just as you have.

Another way to encourage your altruistic and heroic impulses is to change the way you think about *yourself* in relation to the rest of the world. According to the UCLA School of Medicine psychiatrist Jeffrey Schwartz, coauthor of *The Mind and the Brain: Neuroplasticity and the Power of Mental Force*, developing your altruistic capabilities may have a lot to do with how good you are at taking a third-person perspective on your own life. Think about something bad that happened to you recently: maybe your car was stolen, someone close to you died, or your professional reputation took a hit. Now think about a similar bad thing happening to someone else. The more closely your response in the second situation matches your response in the first, the more of a third-person perspective you're able to attain. If you're good at doing this, Schwartz says, you will have "a very different notion of self-other relations, such that the part of your brain you use for making inductions about others you also use for yourself." That means you might make a more effective altruist or hero, because you'll view others' needs the same way you view your own.

One way to attain such a third-person perspective, Schwartz believes, is to start a regimen of mindfulness meditation. While meditating doesn't necessarily equate with becoming altruistic or heroic, it can prepare us to carry out selfless acts like few other practices can. "With mindfulness, you're learning how to direct wise attention," Schwartz says. "Mindfulness is an outer, third-person perspective on first-person experience." As a result of meditation, he says, "you get moral courage. You're just so grounded in your inner awareness and convictions. You're not going to be swayed from doing the right thing." The results of CCARE's compassion cultivation training programs— participants report less fear of showing compassion toward others— support the theory that meditation may encourage selflessness by offering us a perspective on the world that's broader than our default self-centered one.

You can also try breaking out of your default response patterns by training yourself about common rationalizations people use to avoid heroic action. Though in-depth research on the effectiveness of this tactic is still pending, it's one of the main strategies Phil Zimbardo and his colleagues have started using in their heroic education classes. When heroic aspirants learn about the "bystander effect," for instance—the common tendency to shy away from helping people in need when there are other observers in the area—they can more readily recognize this tendency in themselves when it crops up. As a result, they may be better able to consciously set it aside in order to take heroic action when necessary (stepping right up to do the Heimlich maneuver on a choking diner at a restaurant, for instance).

Another key step, according to Zeno Franco, is to mentally carry out the altruistic or heroic acts you're envisioning as accurately as possible. Like a marathon runner, you need to anticipate all the times you're going to be in pain, all the times you're going to suck wind or feel lightheaded, all the times you're going to want to leave your heroic quest by the wayside (like when calling out a rule-breaker puts you in danger of losing your job). "That's how I see the heroic imagination—a visualization process through which one imagines a variety of scenarios as the pressure increases," Franco says. "As likely as it is that you're going to want to exit the situation, how are you going to steel yourself?"

Franco's take on how to prepare yourself for a heroic life is bolstered by ample historical evidence of cut-and-dried or implicit moral codes that detail how to behave in situations where help is needed or lives or principles are threatened. The Navy SEALs, for instance, have such a code. So do many skydivers, which may help explain why Dave Hartsock was able to act heroically in Shirley Dygert's moment of need—he and other skydiving instructors have resolved to themselves that they will put their students' safety ahead of their own in dangerous circumstances. The tradition of a heroic code is a deeply rooted one: According to Clinton Albertson, author of *Anglo-Saxon Saints and Heroes*, such a code was preeminent in Old English society, which glorified "the strong, enterprising chieftain and his courageous band of followers. The essential cohesive elements were the personal loyalty of the retainers and the large-hearted liberality and bold strength of the leader." In a Kennesaw State University study, the presence of a clearly defined company code of ethics strengthened respondents' beliefs that they and other employees were behaving morally and also increased their sense that they would be supported for behaving ethically. It appears, then, that adherence to carefully chosen moral codes may directly influence how we act.

In previous generations, as David Brooks relates in his seminal *Atlantic Monthly* piece "The Organization Kid," moral codes that demanded sacrifice to causes larger than any individual were ubiquitous and spoken of openly. Many of the metaphors applied to heroic behavior were martial ones: People talked about fighting for causes of righteousness. "One more thing must be said about the chivalric code of that era, at least as it was articulated," Brooks writes. "The conflict that educators of the time talked about more than any other was internal conflict, between the good and the evil in each of us."

This is the kind of internal conflict we tend to shy away from discussing these days; it makes us squirm, in part because of its historically religious overtones. But whatever your religious background (or lack thereof), it's essential to consider—as Henderson's corporate heroism trainees and Matt Langdon's Hero Camp kids do—what principles make up your own moral code and what measures you're willing to take to ensure that it's upheld. Depending on your outlook, that may mean getting yourself out of bed every Saturday morning, without fail, to tutor disadvantaged middle school kids. It may mean always putting your students' well-being ahead of your own, as Dave Hartsock did, if you're teaching them a risky skill, or it may mean being willing to die in the service of your country. It may mean all of the above. It may be inspired by the moral codes of organizations to which you belong, or it may be a pastiche of everything you've ever learned about what constitutes selfless behavior. But the bottom line is that without a clearly defined ideal to train your sights on, it's more difficult to set heroic goals and to hold yourself accountable for reaching them.

As you progress toward the outsized goal of molding yourself into a more heroic person, keep reminding yourself that you don't need to pull off high-stakes rescue attempts or garner widespread recognition in order to make genuine progress. It may actually be better to start small—giving a modest donation to charity, volunteering for an hour or two a week—so that the giving-related pleasure response in your brain won't initially be drowned out by undue aversion at the thought of parting with substantial money or time. Over time, you can progress to higher levels of self-sacrifice. This is one of the selflessness credos that comforts me the most.

Would-be heroes' personal initiative plays by far the largest role in shaping their developing identity as über-altruists. But as social scientists, enterprising marketers, and others have shown, it's also possible to create conditions for altruism to emerge not just by specifically training people to be more unselfish, but by nudging them into unselfishness by manipulating various aspects of their environment. Yale's Laurie Santos points out that such a "nudge" approach, popularized by the lawyer Cass Sunstein and the economist Richard Thaler, could be used to develop the selflessness equivalent of "get out of jail free" cards: ways for people to behave more altruistically without it feeling like work. "Given that we have certain social goals," Santos says, "why don't we set up architectures in a way that gets people to do what they'd like their choices to be naturally?"

One crafty way to do this is to take advantage of the innate human tendency to preserve the status quo. Countries where people are designated as organ donors unless they opt out, for example, typically boast higher donation rates than countries that require applicants to opt in to donor programs. Another example is the Yahoo-powered accessory search engine goodsearch.com, which gives 50 percent of its advertising revenue to charities that users specify individually. Users must consciously opt to use Goodsearch as opposed to Bing or Google, but they can use it just as they would any other search application.

Erecting pro-altruism architectures on a major level will require some social or political consensus about what those architectures should look like. That way, people won't be manipulated without their consent; instead, the architectures will act more as reminders, gentle probes that steer them back to the way they say they want to behave. Imagine a system where the government would assume citizens wished to give 10 percent of their income to a charity of their choice. They could choose to opt out, but just as in the organ donor scenario, total charitable contributions would likely be much higher than they are now. On a smaller scale, heads of schools could require all graduates to complete a certain number of hours of volunteer service, and heads of companies could set up incentives for employees to serve the community—for instance, by offering bonuses or status perks to workers who participate in outreach efforts.

While most philosophical traditions consider altruism and heroism to be outgrowths of a certain kind of inherent moral character, the interesting thing about strategies like these is that their success doesn't require participants to evolve morally. They involve a change in the environment, not a change in the human *actors* in the environment. Such interventions may represent the converse of Abu Ghraib and the Stanford Prison Experiment: If humans have the potential to act like demons in situations that encourage moral deterioration, they can also act like angels in situations that encourage altruistic behavior—all without copious amounts of moral searching or reflection involved.

Cultivating a truly heroic existence is easiest when you have both social support and an unquenchable intrinsic motivation. In the end, succeeding at your altruistic goals comes down to keeping them at the forefront of your mind when so many other responsibilities and concerns continually clamor for your attention. When your to-do list is crammed with items like "empty dishwasher," "refinance house," and "retrieve kids from day care," it can be difficult to remember that there was a time when you resolved to better the world outside the limited sphere of your own home, job, and family.

But the ever-looming nearsightedness of self-focus doesn't change the scope of suffering in the wider world, and it doesn't alter the limited amount of time we have to put our ideals into practice. In the movie *Dead Poets Society*, Robin Williams's character, the English teacher John Keating, has his students gaze at a wall of black-and-white photos of previous school graduates who have since passed on, noting that they are all now dead in the ground. "Did they wait until it was too late to make from their lives even one iota of what they were capable?" he asks the students. "If you listen real close, you can hear them whisper their legacy to you. Go on, lean in. Listen, you hear it?—Carpe—hear it?—*Carpe, carpe diem.*"

While the stakes are certainly high for each of us as individuals—did we succeed in making of ourselves the most of which we were capable?—they are even higher for the planet as a whole. The opportunities for heroism and altruism are almost too abundant to be believed, provided we're willing to broaden our focus long enough to truly see and understand them.

And therein lies perhaps the most important key to leading an altruistic life: having the courage to see beyond the particular circumstances of our own existence. The political philosopher John Rawls advocated stepping back and taking a "veil of ignorance" approach: What would we want the world to be like—how would we want it to function—if we could not know in advance what our particular talents, handicaps, and economic and social station in life were going to be?

The stakes became very clear for Christoph von Toggenburg early in life. As a young man, he took a year to travel around the world and spent time in India, where he visited an institution in Calcutta designed to help the poor. In the midst of all the human suffering, he met tireless volunteers who ministered to every person who came through the doors, treating them not as pieces of refuse off the street, but as human beings like any other. The whole experience fueled his desire to do whatever he could to help people in dire straits. The need, he knew, was simply too great not to. "My decision was extremely conscious," he says. "When you have the energy, I see it as a responsibility. People need the kind of person who stands up and says, 'No, I do not accept this.'"

Like Zimbardo, Franco, and Doty, von Toggenburg sees the heroic and altruistic paths as open to anyone who chooses to pursue them— regardless of their innate talents and abilities or where they find themselves in life. "With many of the people I have known over time, they do not see themselves as heroes, but they are *made* heroes. They see it's something that they need, too." What sustains him is that he has managed to catch and hold on to one of the most commonly overlooked truths: What we need and what the world needs are very often one and the same. Great thinkers and writers have long said so, and researchers are accumulating evidence that underscores it. Armed with such hard-won knowledge, what excuse do any of us have to hold back from fulfilling our heroic destiny?

Acknowledgments

It's fitting that this book came into being through the selfless contributions of so many. I am grateful to everyone at Stanford's Center for Compassion and Altruism Research and Education (CCARE) and the Heroic Imagination Project (HIP) for giving me an incomparable firsthand look at what they were up to. Phil Zimbardo, Clint Wilkins, Brooke Deterline, Jim Doty, Kelly McGonigal, Leah Weiss Ekstrom, et al.—without your time, openness, and enthusiasm, this project could never have gotten off the ground. Also, thanks to Bill Harbaugh for taking me up on my wacky request for a brain scan and for giving me a lift to Telluride.

Joe Veltre, thank you for believing in this idea when it was nothing more than an inkling in my mind—and for helping me turn that inkling into something bigger than I could have imagined. You, too, Courtney Young. I'm glad we got to work together even if it was only for a short time. Thanks to my intrepid succession of editors at Current: Jillian Gray, Eric Meyers, and Maria Gagliano. Your contributions made this a better book every step of the way. John McGhee provided sharp-eyed copyediting support to save me from foot-in-mouth moments.

A thousand thanks to my beta readers, including Kara Gennis,

ACKNOWLEDGMENTS

Adelaide Svoboda, Bill Hallahan, and Mason Inman. Your thoughtful feedback and gentle corrections gave me confidence that this book would be at its best before it headed out into the world.

Thanks to my family and friends, who listened and asked questions, inspiring me to explore new aspects of heroism and altruism. Special shout-outs to Jerry, Adelaide, and Mark Svoboda for their love and support; Jerry Svoboda Sr.; Ellen and Lew Hollmeyer; Guido Arnout, who asked how the book was coming along whenever I saw him (and lent me his library of books on related topics); Val and Mark Werness; Geoff Lister, Kathy Hiltunen and family; Roshni Ray Ricchetti, my compatriot in baby-wrangling, and her husband, Bryan; Brent Werness and Jessica Chong; Kara and Jamie Gennis; Katie and Jim Herman; Dalia Rawson Hughes and Gareth Hughes; Viet-Tam Luu and Janice Nimer; Rebecca and Andy Ritger; Sarah and Pat Greene; Jyoti Kandlikar Patel; John Boccacino; Pat O'Neill; Brandon Shroyer; Philip Ostromogolsky; Rebecca Mendelson; Lucas Matthews, for sending articles; and Shannon McIntyre, my forever friend since seventh grade, and her husband, Andy.

I am indebted to everyone associated with California Community Partners for Youth—staff, mentors, volunteers, and kids. I'm certain that my involvement with CCPY over the past six years helped lead me to my decision to write this book. Jeff Bornefeld, Liset Morales, Hilda Morales, Pattie Cortese, Amanda Bunnell, Nicole Branscome, Tom and Karen Ryan, Casey Powers, Ade Faison, Bubba Murnan, all of my mentees through the years, and so many more—you all inspire me more than you know.

Finally, thanks to my husband, Eric Werness, who worked from home while bouncing our baby boy on his lap so I could get my own work done, picked up the dish-rinsing and diaper-changing slack when I was riveted to my laptop, read my manuscript when he could have been watching *Mythbusters*, and reminded me that everything was going to be all right. You are my hero—today and always.

Notes

INTRODUCTION: CAN ANYONE BECOME A HERO?

Page

1 **It was a sunny summer day just outside Houston:** My description of what happened the day Dave Hartsock and Shirley Dygert's tandem skydive went wrong is based primarily on an in-person interview with both of them on September 15, 2010.

4 **As Wesley Autrey did when he jumped off a New York City subway platform:** Cara Buckley, "Man Is Rescued by Stranger on Subway Tracks," *New York Times*, January 3, 2007.

4 **The architect of the famed Stanford Prison Experiment:** Philip Zimbardo, in-person interview, September 2, 2010.

5 **he wanted to understand what people really thought qualified as heroism:** Zeno Franco, Kathy Blau, and Philip Zimbardo, "Heroism: A Conceptual Analysis and Differentiation Between Heroic Action and Altruism," *Review of General Psychology* 15, no. 2 (2011): 99–113.

6 **So is Ted Johnson, the former New England Patriots linebacker:** Jackie MacMullen," 'I Don't Want Anyone to End Up Like Me': Plagued by Post-concussion Syndrome and Battling an Amphetamine Addiction, Former Patriots Linebacker Ted Johnson Is a Shell of His Former Self," *Boston Globe*, February 2, 2007. Accessed December 10, 2012, from http://www.boston.com /sports/articles/2007/02/02/i_dont_want_anyone_to_end_up_like_me.

6 **"Social heroism has potential to create real change":** Zeno Franco, phone interview, July 14, 2011.

9 **The political theorist Hannah Arendt's doctrine of the "banality of evil":** Hannah Arendt, *Eichmann in Jerusalem: A Report on the Banality of Evil* (New York: Viking Press, 1963).

CHAPTER ONE: IN THE GENES?

13 **Krom was thirsty, and it seemed like there was nothing she could do:** This summary was composed with the help of information from Frans De Waal, *Our Inner Ape: A Leading Primatologist Explains Why We Are Who We Are* (New York: Penguin, 2006).

14 **Anuradha Koirala once came home every day to a partner who hit her:** My synopsis of Anuradha Koirala's life and personal journey owes much to Ebonne Ruffins's report "Rescuing Girls from Sex Slavery," CNN, April 30, 2010. Accessed December 10, 2012, from http://www.cnn.com/2010/LIVING/04/29 /cnnheroes.koirala.nepal/index.html.

15 **Bonobos come to the aid of other injured bonobos:** Nahoko Tokuyama et al., "Bonobos Apparently Search for a Lost Member Injured by a Snare," *Primates* 53, no. 3 (July 2012): 215–19.

15 **ravens call to other members of their species:** Bernd Heinrich, *Ravens in Winter* (New York: Vintage, 1991).

15 **meerkats stand guard to allow others in the pack:** Mico Tatalovic, "Evolution of Raised Guarding Behavior in Meerkats, *Suricata suricatta*," *Journal of Young Investigators* 20 (2010).

15 **Eighteen-month-old toddlers in a study:** Felix Warneken and Michael Tomasello, "Altruistic Helping in Human Infants and Young Chimpanzees," *Science* 311, no. 5765 (2006): 1301–3.

15 **A cursory read of Darwinian evolutionary doctrine:** Charles Darwin, *On the Origin of Species by Means of Natural Selection* (New York: D. Appleton and Company, 1869).

16 **Honeybees, though, gave him pause:** Lee Dugatkin, *The Altruism Equation: Seven Scientists Search for the Origins of Goodness* (Princeton, NJ: Princeton University Press, 2006). My historical descriptions in this chapter—particularly of the lives and theories of Charles Darwin, Peter Kropotkin, and W. D. Hamilton—are indebted to Dugatkin's book, the most comprehensive exploration I've seen of the history of scientific thought about altruism.

17 **"I saw mutual aid and mutual support carried on to an extent" and "There is an immense amount of warfare and extermination going on amidst var-**

ious species": Peter Kropotkin, *Mutual Aid: A Factor of Evolution* (London: William Heinemann, 1902).

18 **He structured this rule as $r \times b > c$:** John Cartwright, *Evolution and Human Behavior: Darwinian Perspectives on Human Nature* (Cambridge, MA: MIT Press, 2000).

18 **In 1981, the University of Cape Town zoologist Jenny Jarvis:** Jenny Jarvis, "Eusociality in a Mammal: Cooperative Breeding in Naked Mole-Rat Colonies," *Science*, May 1, 1981: 571–73.

19 **About a decade later, the Cornell biologist Hudson Reeve:** Hudson K. Reeve et al., "DNA 'Fingerprinting' Reveals High Levels of Inbreeding in Colonies of the Eusocial Naked Mole-Rat," *Proceedings of the National Academy of Sciences*, April 1990: 2496–500.

19 **Take the case of William Muir, an animal breeder:** David Sloan Wilson, "Truth and Reconciliation for Group Selection XIV: Group Selection in the Laboratory." *The Huffington Post*, August 23, 2009. Accessed May 10, 2013, from http://www.huffingtonpost.com/david-sloan-wilson/truth-and-reconciliation_b_266316.html. See also James Craig and William Muir, "Genetics and the Behavior of Chickens: Welfare and Productivity," in *Genetics and the Behavior of Domestic Animals*, ed. Temple Grandin, 263-98.

20 **"They were not spending energy competing":** The Charles Goodnight quotes in this chapter come from a phone interview with him on April 28, 2011.

21 **Using genes from sources such as algae and pond scum:** My description of Karl Deisseroth's work exploring the neural origins of prosociality is based mainly on the presentation he gave at the "Scientific Explorations of Compassion and Altruism" conference presented by the Center for Compassion and Altruism Research and Education, Stanford University, October 15, 2010.

22 **the neuroscientist Jordan Grafman has investigated specific regions of the human brain:** My take on Jordan Grafman's brain research was gleaned from an in-person interview with him on July 19, 2011.

23 **Grafman and his colleagues recruited nineteen study subjects:** The study to which I refer in this section is Jorge Moll, Jordan Grafman, et al., "Human Fronto-Mesolimbic Networks Guide Decisions About Charitable Donation," *Proceedings of the National Academy of Sciences* 103, no. 42 (October 17, 2006): 15623–28.

24 **In a separate experiment by the Claremont Graduate University neuro-economist Paul Zak:** Paul J. Zak et al., "Oxytocin Increases Generosity in Humans," *PLoS ONE* 2, no. 11: e1128.

25 **The University of Wisconsin neuroscientist Michael Koenigs and his colleagues:** Michael Koenigs, Antonio Damasio, et al., "Damage to the Prefrontal

Cortex Increases Utilitarian Moral Judgements," *Nature* 446, no. 7138 (April 19, 2007): 908–11.

26 **A part of the prefrontal cortex may also encourage unselfishness:** Jamil Zaki, "Cognitive and Neural Sources of Prosociality," public talk, Stanford University, January 24, 2012.

28 **"The biological isn't meant to explain everything":** Judith Lichtenberg, phone interview, October 27, 2011.

CHAPTER TWO: THE ECONOMICS OF UNSELFISHNESS

31 **The well-known philosopher and economist John Stuart Mill:** John Stuart Mill, *Essays on Some Unsettled Questions of Political Economy* (London: Longmans, Green, Reader, and Dyer, 1844).

32 **The University of Oregon economist exudes an offbeat charm:** Several personal tidbits about Harbaugh are chronicled on his official homepage. Accessed December 11, 2012, from http://harbaugh.uoregon.edu. Bill Harbaugh reflections and quotes in this chapter are from phone and in-person interviews with him in 2011 and 2012.

32 **In 2011, Americans gave a staggering $298.3 billion:** "Charitable Giving Statistics: Total Giving 2001–2011," National Philanthropic Trust. Accessed December 11, 2012, from http://www.nptrust.org/philanthropic-resources /charitable-giving-statistics.

33 **Back in the 1970s, for instance, the Cornell psychology student William Upton:** William Upton, *Altruism, Attribution, and Intrinsic Motivation in the Recruitment of Blood Donors*, doctoral dissertation, Cornell University, 1973.

33 **In the late 1990s, he studied a group of law school graduates:** William T. Harbaugh, "What Do Donations Buy? A Model of Philanthropy Based on Prestige and Warm Glow," *Journal of Public Economics* 67 (1998): 269–84.

34 **"People take on great risks to help others":** Robb Willer, phone interview, April 25, 2011.

34 **While subjects were in the scanner, a computer monitor in front of them:** The primary study described in this chapter is William T. Harbaugh, Ulrich Mayr, and Daniel R. Burghart, "Neural Responses to Taxation and Voluntary Giving Reveal Motives for Charitable Donations," *Science* 316, no. 5831 (June 15, 2007): 1622–25.

37 **"It's a very intractable question":** Judith Lichtenberg, phone interview, October 27, 2011.

38 **Still, the notion that giving is meaningful even if givers' motives are less than pure:** Peggy Salinger, *Dream Catcher: A Memoir* (New York: Washington Square Press, 2000).

42 **something similar may be happening when people decide to give their time:** Office of Research and Policy Development, Corporation for National and Community Service, "The Health Benefits of Volunteering: A Review of Recent Research." Accessed December 19, 2012, from http://www2.illinois.gov /serve/Documents/Health_Benefits_Volunteering.pdf.

CHAPTER THREE: MENTAL BLOCKS AGAINST HEROISM

45 **Flash back nearly seventy years to 1944:** Anne Frank background material was derived from many rereadings of *Anne Frank: The Diary of a Young Girl.* Trans. B. M. Mooyaart (New York: Doubleday, 1952).

45 **Nearly fifty years later, Zlata Filipović, a young Bosnian girl:** Zlata Filipović, *Zlata's Diary: A Child's Life in Sarajevo* (London: Penguin Books, 1994).

45 **100,000 of her fellow Bosnian citizens were killed:** Minority Rights Group International, *World Directory of Minorities and Indigenous Peoples—Bosnia and Hercegovina: Overview,* October 2011. Accessed December 18, 2012, from http://www.unhcr.org/refworld/docid/4954ce17c.html.

46 **the United States government chose not to initiate military strikes:** Michael Berenbaum, "Why the Allies Didn't Bomb the Death Camps," blog series, britannica.com, April 2–4, 2007. Accessed December 18, 2012, from http://www.britannica.com/blogs/author/mberenbaum.

47 **the United States had knowledge of what was happening in Bosnia:** Ivo H. Daalder, "Decision to Intervene: How the War in Bosnia Ended," *Foreign Service Journal,* December 1998.

47 **The Polish poet Wisława Szymborska once wrote:** Wisława Szymborska, *People on a Bridge: Poems* (London: Forest Books, 1990).

47 **"People are willing to do so much to save individuals":** Elizabeth Svoboda, "The Genocidal Blind Spot," *Science & Spirit* 18, no. 2 (May–June 2007).

47 **Slovic is the president of Decision Research:** Most of Paul Slovic's quotes and reflections in this chapter are from an in-person interview with him on June 14, 2011.

48 **The theory essentially states that when stimuli get more intense:** Daniel Kahneman and Amos Tversky, "Advances in Prospect Theory: Cumulative Representation of Uncertainty," *Journal of Risk and Uncertainty* 5, no. 4 (October 1992).

49 **They told experimental participants a story about a grant-funding agency:** Paul Slovic et al., "Insensitivity to the Value of Human Life: A Study of Psychophysical Numbing," *Journal of Risk and Uncertainty* 14, no. 3 (February 1997).

50 **Some participants in the study were given $5:** Deborah Small, George Loewenstein, and Paul Slovic, "Sympathy and Callousness: The Impact of Delibera-

tive Thought on Donations to Identifiable and Statistical Victims," *Organizational Behavior and Human Decision Processes* 102, no. 2 (2007): 143–53.

51 **supplied certain subjects with children's names, ages, and pictures:** Tehila Kogut and Ilana Ritov, "The 'Identified Victim' Effect: An Identified Group, or Just a Single Individual?" *Journal of Behavioral Decision Making* 18, no. 3 (2005): 157–67.

51 **To see if this generosity-dilution effect held true:** Paul Slovic, "If I Look at the Mass I Will Never Act: Psychic Numbing and Genocide," International Library of Ethics, Law and Technology 5, *Emotions and Risky Technologies* (2010): 37–59.

51 **The two researchers asked subjects to read a story:** Daryl Cameron and Keith Payne, "Escaping Affect: How Motivated Emotion Regulation Creates Insensitivity to Mass Suffering," *Journal of Personality and Social Psychology* 100, no. 1 (2011): 1–15.

52 **"Probably at least sometimes people don't know they're doing it":** Keith Payne, phone interview, September 22, 2011.

52 **this principle of basic human equality is even codified:** United Nations, "The Universal Declaration of Human Rights." Accessed December 19, 2012, from http://www.un.org/en/documents/udhr/index.shtml.

54 **"Maweu is 45 years old, married and has three children":** "Maweu from Kenya," Kiva loan webpage. Accessed December 17, 2012, from http://www.kiva.org/lend/379193.

54 **Another aspiring entrepreneur, Leliosa, age thirty-five:** "Leliosa from Philippines," Kiva loan webpage. Accessed December 17, 2012, from http://www.kiva.org/lend/379068.

54 **Since its inception, Kiva has supplied:** "Latest Statistics," Kiva webpage. Accessed December 17, 2012, from http:// www.kiva.org/about/stats.

55 **"My job as a journalist is to find these larger issues":** Krista Tippett, "Nicholas Kristof on Journalism and Compassion," *On Being*, September 23, 2010. Accessed December 17, 2012, from http://www.onbeing.org/program/journalism-and-compassion/transcript/956.

56 **17.7 percent quit school before graduating:** "State Schools Chief Tom Torlakson Reports Climb in Graduation Rates for California Students," California Department of Education news release, June 27, 2012. Accessed December 17, 2012, from http://www.cde.ca.gov/nr/ne/yr12/yr12rel65.asp.

CHAPTER FOUR: INNER FOCUS AND COMPASSIONATE ACTION

59 **In a classroom at Stanford University's Li Ka Shing Center:** The first-person narration in this chapter is based on my experience taking the Compassion Cultivation Training class at Stanford University in Spring 2012.

61 **"Sometimes I might sit down beside someone":** Etty Hillesum, *An Interrupted Life and Letters from Westerbork* (New York: Henry Holt, 1996).

61 **One pioneer in this new field of meditation science:** Quotes from Richard Davidson in this chapter and background regarding his work are primarily based on my in-person interview with him on February 10, 2012.

62 **To begin with, he invited a French Buddhist monk:** John Geirland, "Buddha on the Brain," *Wired*, February 2006. Accessed December 18, 2012, from http://www.wired.com/wired/archive/14.02/dalai.html.

63 **Encouraged by these results, Davidson decided to probe more deeply:** Richard Davidson, J. A. Brefczynski-Lewis, et al., "Regulation of the Neural Circuitry of Emotion by Compassion Meditation: Effects of Meditative Expertise," *PLOS One* 3, no. 3: e1897. Accessed January 10, 2013, from http://www.plosone.org/article/fetchArticle.action?articleURI=info:doi/10.1371/journal.pone.0001897#abstract0.

64 **But Davidson's findings have not met with universal acclaim:** John Geirland, "Buddha on the Brain," *Wired*, February 2006. Accessed December 18, 2012, from http://www.wired.com/wired/archive/14.02/dalai.html.

67 **When the Stanford psychologist Jeanne Tsai . . . gave meditators:** Jeanne Tsai, presentation, "Scientific Explorations of Compassion and Altruism," conference presented by the Center for Compassion and Altruism Research and Education, Stanford University, October 15, 2010; and follow-up e-mail with collaborator Birgit Koopmann-Holm.

68 **Meanwhile, Tsai's Stanford colleagues—the researchers Hooria Jazaieri, Philippe Goldin, and others:** Hooria Jazaieri, Philippe Goldin, et al., "Enhancing Compassion: A Randomized Controlled Trial of a Compassion Cultivation Training Program," *Journal of Happiness Studies*, published online July 25, 2012. Accessed December 19, 2012, from spl.stanford.edu/pdfs/2012%20Jazaieri%20JOHS.pdf.

68 **participants testified that CCT helped awaken their feelings of affinity:** Leah Weiss Ekstrom, presentation, 2012 Science of Compassion conference, Telluride, CO.

69 **following a similar compassion meditation course at Emory University:** Jennifer Mascaro et al., "Compassion Meditation Enhances Empathic Accuracy and Related Neural Activity," *Social Cognitive and Affective Neuroscience*,

2012. Accessed December 19, 2012, from http://scan.oxfordjournals.org/con
tent/early/2012/09/28/scan.nss095.full.pdf.

69 **Compassion meditators in an Emory study who had higher-than-average
practice times:** Thaddeus Pace et al., "Effect of Compassion Meditation on
Neuroendocrine, Innate Immune and Behavioral Responses to Psychosocial
Stress," *Psychoneuroendocrinology* 34, no. 1 (2009): 87–98.

69 **the scientific vocabulary needed to make such a determination is still
being refined:** Emiliana Simon-Thomas, phone interview, March 22, 2012.

70 **There's intriguing new evidence that they may actually do so:** Helen Y.
Weng, Andrew S. Fox, et al. "Compassion Training Alters Altruism and Neural
Responses to Suffering." *Psychological Science*, May 21, 2013.

70 **"This meets huge needs. It isn't fringe anymore":** Leah Weiss Ekstrom, in-
person interview, March 7, 2012.

72 **the main character Danny's rabbi father raises him in near-silence:** Chaim
Potok, *The Chosen* (New York: Simon & Schuster, 1967).

CHAPTER FIVE: SUFFERING AND HEROISM

75 **For some people, school memories prompt a wave of rose-tinted nostalgia:**
My telling of Jodee Blanco's story, woven through this chapter, is based primarily on my phone interview with her, September 15, 2011.

77 **"When we feel wretched, that softens us up:** Pema Chodron, *When Things
Fall Apart: Heart Advice for Difficult Times* (Boston: Shambhala Publications,
2005).

78 **when the researcher Pilar Hernandez-Wolfe examined the lives:** Pilar
Hernandez-Wolfe, "Altruism Born of Suffering: How Colombian Human Rights
Activists Transform Pain Into Prosocial Action," *Journal of Humanistic Psychology*, September 1, 2010. Accessed December 14, 2012, from http://jhp.sagepub
.com/content/early/2010/08/30/0022167810379960.abstract.

79 **Miep Gies, who helped Anne Frank's family hide from the Nazis:** Miep
Gies, "A Note by Miep Gies," in Melissa Muller, *Anne Frank: The Biography*
(New York: Henry Holt, 1998).

80 **No researcher has delved more deeply into the connection:** My account of
Ervin Staub's life story and research is based primarily on my phone interview
with him, September 13, 2011, and subsequent e-mail.

80 **Raoul Wallenberg, a secretary at Budapest's Swedish legation:** "Raoul Wallenberg and the Rescue of Jews in Budapest," United States Holocaust Memorial
Museum. Accessed December 17, 2012, from http://www.ushmm.org/wlc/en
/article.php?ModuleId=10005211.

82 **When the social scientist Zora Raboteg-Šarić and her colleagues studied:**

Zora Raboteg-Šarić et al., "War and Children's Aggressive and Prosocial Behaviour," *European Journal of Personality*, September 1994: 201–12.

82 **When the Indiana University of Pennsylvania psychologist Krys Kaniasty studied:** Krys Kaniasty and Fran Norris, "In Search of Altruistic Community: Patterns of Social Support Mobilization Following Hurricane Hugo," *American Journal of Community Psychology*, August 1995: 447–77. Accessed November 30, 2012, from http://www.ncbi.nlm.nih.gov/pubmed/8546107.

82 **He and his colleague Johanna Vollhardt asked subjects whether they'd ever been victims:** Ervin Staub and Johanna Vollhardt, "Inclusive Altruism Born of Suffering: The Relationship Between Adversity and Prosocial Attitudes and Behavior Toward Disadvantaged Outgroups," *American Journal of Orthopsychiatry*, July 2011: 307–15. Accessed November 30, 2012, from http://www.ncbi.nlm.nih.gov/pubmed/21729011.

84 **The psychiatrist Viktor Frankl, who was deported from Czechoslovakia:** Viktor Frankl, *Man's Search for Meaning* (New York: Beacon Press, 1959).

84 **Staub has had his students write a variety of autobiographical papers:** Ervin Staub, "The Roots of Goodness: The Fulfillment of Basic Human Needs and the Development of Caring, Helping and Non-Aggression, Inclusive Caring, Moral Courage, Active Bystandership, and Altruism Born of Suffering," in G. Carlo and C. Edwards, eds., *Moral Motivation Through the Life Span* (Lincoln: University of Nebraska Press, 2005). Accessed November 30, 2012, from people.umass.edu/estaub/The_Roots_of_Goodness.pdf.

86 **members of the economic lower class are more likely to act altruistically:** Paul Piff, Dacher Keltner, et al., "Having Less, Giving More: The Influence of Social Class on Prosocial Behavior," *Journal of Personality and Social Psychology* 99, no. 5 (November 2010): 771–84.

86 **"When you face uncertainty, it makes you orient to other people":** Dacher Keltner, in-person interview, August 10, 2011.

CHAPTER SIX: HELPING, HEALTH, AND HAPPINESS

89 **Mike Hrostoski found himself hitting a major lull:** My account of Mike Hrostoski's summer volunteer trip and the insights he gained is based primarily on my phone interview with him, July 11, 2012.

91 **they don't shock Allan Luks in the slightest:** My account of Allan Luks's life and work in this chapter is based on my in-person interview with him, June 12, 2012, as well as on the book he wrote with Peggy Payne, *The Healing Power of Doing Good: The Health and Spiritual Benefits of Helping Others* (New York: Fawcett Columbine, 1991).

92 **The United Way reported a severe shortage of mentors for at-risk students:**

NOTES

Mark Price, "United Way Seeks 1,000 Mentors for Kids," *Charlotte Observer*, May 17, 2012. Accessed November 28, 2012, from http://www.charlotteobserver.com/2012/05/17/3246041/united-way-seeks-1000-mentors.html.

92 **a volunteer ambulance service in central New York State was recently forced to shut down:** Angela Hong, "Volunteer Shortage Closes NY Ambulance Service," WHAM, May 8, 2012. Accessed November 28, 2012, from http://www.ems1.com/volunteer-rural-ems/articles/1283629-volunteer-shortage-closes-NY-ambulance-service.

94 **Frank Riessman published an article in the journal *Social Work:*** Frank Riessman, "The 'Helper' Therapy Principle," *Social Work* 10, no. 2 (1965): 27–32. See also Stephen G. Post, "Updating the Helper Therapy Principle," *Psychology Today*, September 3, 2008.

95 **Schwartz . . . and her colleagues divided multiple sclerosis patients into two groups:** Carolyn Schwartz and Meir Sendor, "Helping Others Helps Oneself: Response Shift Effects in Peer Support," *Social Science & Medicine* 48, no. 11 (June 1999): 1563–75.

96 **"These people seemed to be blossoming":** Carolyn Schwartz quotes and observations in this chapter are from my phone interview with her, June 28, 2012.

96 **Alcoholics Anonymous members who were helping other addicts:** Maria Pagano et al., "Helping Other Alcoholics in Alcoholics Anonymous and Drinking Outcomes: Findings from Project MATCH," *Journal of Studies on Alcohol*, November 2004: 766–73. Accessed December 11, 2012, from http://www.ncbi.nlm.nih.gov/pubmed/15700515.

96 **a 2010 survey of more than 4,500 volunteers:** UnitedHealthcare, "Volunteering and Your Health: How Giving Back Benefits Everyone." Accessed November 28, 2012, from www.unitedhealthgroup.com/news/rel2010/UHC-VolunteerMatch-Survey-Fact-Sheet.pdf.

96 **a 2012 study of older Maori and non-Maori in New Zealand:** Patrick Dulin et al., "Volunteering Predicts Happiness Among Older Māori and non-Māori in the New Zealand Health, Work, and Retirement Longitudinal Study," *Aging & Mental Health* 16, no. 5 (2012): 617–24.

96 **frequent volunteers had a 19 percent lower mortality risk:** Alex H. S. Harris and Carl E. Thoresen, "Volunteering Is Associated with Delayed Mortality in Older People: Analysis of the Longitudinal Study of Aging," *Journal of Health Psychology* 10, no. 6 (2005): 739–52.

96 **University of Michigan researchers studied 423 older couples who were followed for five years:** Stephanie Brown et al., "Providing Social Support May Be More Beneficial Than Receiving It: Results from a Prospective Study of Mortality," *Psychological Science* 14, no. 4 (July 2003): 320–27.

218

97 **Lyubomirsky wanted to test the connection in a real-world setting:** Sonja Lyubomirsky et al., "Pursuing Happiness: The Architecture of Sustainable Change," *Review of General Psychology* 9, no. 2 (2005): 111–31.

97 **"It could be there's a very short":** Francesca Borgonovi, phone interview, July 6, 2012.

97 **Helping others may signal our bodies to release pleasurable chemicals:** Sara Konrath, "The Power of Philanthropy and Volunteering," in Felicia Huppert and Cary Cooper, eds., *Interventions and Policies to Enhance Wellbeing* (Hoboken, NJ: Wiley, 2012).

97 **The boost we get from helping may also mute our stress response:** Stephen G. Post, "It's Good to Be Good: 2011 5th Annual Scientific Report on Health, Happiness, and Helping Others," *International Journal of Person Centered Medicine* 1, no. 4: 814–29.

97 **"Evolution suggests that human nature evolved emotionally":** Stephen G. Post, "Updating the Helper Therapy Principle," *Psychology Today*, September 3, 2008. Accessed November 28, 2012, from http://www.psychologytoday.com /blog/the-joy-giving/200809/updating-the-helper-therapy-principle.

98 **What kinds of helping are most likely to lead to lasting satisfaction?:** Jonathan Haidt observation and description of my casual experiment are based on Elizabeth Svoboda, "Pay It Forward," *Psychology Today*, July 2006. Accessed December 19, 2012, from http://www.psychologytoday.com/articles/200607/pay-it-forward.

98 **"When I started with Elijah, they tell you":** James Frank, phone interview, July 11, 2012.

99 **people who experienced the most significant longevity benefits:** Sara Konrath, Stephanie Brown, et al., "Motives for Volunteering Are Associated with Mortality Risk in Older Adults," *Health Psychology* 31, no. 1 (2012): 87–96.

101 **"I think, 'I cannot do one more thing'":** Victoria Trabosh, phone interview, July 11, 2012.

102 **"Doing something nice gives you more happiness bang for your buck . . ."** Laurie Santos, in-person interview, July 20, 2011.

CHAPTER SEVEN: THE SCIENTIFIC SEARCH FOR ALTRUISM

105 **It's a warm fall day at Stanford University:** I witnessed these proceedings at the "Scientific Explorations of Compassion and Altruism" conference presented by the Center for Compassion and Altruism Research and Education, Stanford University, October 15, 2010.

107 **Recently, many of these discussions have revolved:** My descriptions of James Doty's life and work in this chapter are based primarily on in-person and phone interviews with him, 2010–2012.

110 **Phil Zimbardo was starting his own related venture:** Zimbardo told me the story of how HIP got started in an in-person interview, September 2, 2010.

111 **He recruited twenty-four normal college students:** Philip Zimbardo, "The Stanford Prison Experiment: A Simulation Study of the Psychology of Imprisonment." Accessed November 28, 2012, from http://www.prisonexp.org.

114 **More than three hundred people make the trek to the mountains:** "The Science of Compassion" conference presented by the Center for Compassion and Altruism Research and Education, Telluride, CO, July 22–25, 2012.

116 **One typical HIP informational event:** Narration in this section is based on my observation of Philip Zimbardo, "Inspiring Heroic Leadership in the Boardroom & Senior Management," talk given at Stanford University Rock Center for Corporate Governance, May 9, 2012.

119 **"This is a field that has been populated by true believers":** Dan Gilgoff, "Can Meditation Change Your Brain? Contemplative Neuroscientists Believe It Can," CNN, October 26, 2010. Accessed December 3, 2012, from http://religion.blogs.cnn.com/2010/10/26/can-meditation-change-your-brain-contemplative-neuroscientists-believe-it-can.

120 **Most scientists try to avoid the appearance of bias:** A similar line of critique was advanced by John Geirland, "Buddha on the Brain," *Wired*, February 2006. Accessed December 18, 2012, from http://www.wired.com/wired/archive/14.02/dalai.html.

121 **The John Templeton Foundation, established in 1987:** "Foundation at a Glance," John Templeton Foundation. Accessed December 3, 2012, from http://www.templeton.org/who-we-are/about-the-foundation/foundation-at-a-glance.

CHAPTER EIGHT: HEROES IN TRAINING

125 **The ARISE charter high school near downtown Oakland:** My narration of classroom proceedings in this chapter is based on my observation of the Heroic Imagination Project afternoon workshop, ARISE High School, November 17, 2010.

125 **Kitty Genovese, a white woman from New York City:** "Queens Woman Is Stabbed to Death in Front of Home," *New York Times*, March 14, 1964: 26.

126 **the larger the number of bystanders who witness an emergency situation:** Richard A. Griggs, *Psychology: A Concise Introduction* (New York: Worth Publishers, 2012).

127 **the 2009 police shooting of Oscar Grant on the BART transit system:** Demian Bulwa et al., "Protests over BART Shooting Turn Violent," *San Francisco Chronicle*, January 8, 2009. Accessed December 11, 2012, from http:

//www.sfgate.com/bayarea/article/Protests-over-BART-shooting-turn-violent
-3255351.php.

128 **In the so-called Good Samaritan experiment:** John Darley and C. Daniel Batson, " 'From Jerusalem to Jericho': A Study of Situational and Dispositional Variables in Helping Behavior," *Journal of Personality and Social Psychology* 27 (1973): 100–108.

129 **"Heroism, like altruism, is sociocentric":** Philip Zimbardo, Skype interview, September 24, 2012.

129 **Jerry Sternin, who was saddled with the seemingly insoluble problem:** Positive Deviance Initiative, "Spotlight Case Study: Vietnam as a Prototype for the PD Approach." Accessed November 29, 2012, from www.positivedeviance .org/about_pd/case_studies.html.

131 **Wilkins plans to turn a polished version of HIP's education curriculum into a revenue stream:** Clint Wilkins provided background information and observations about HIP's education programs for this chapter in in-person and phone interviews, 2010–2012.

132 **Matt Langdon, a heroism educator based in Brighton, Michigan:** This section is based primarily on in-person interviews with Matt Langdon, June 29–30, 2011, and on my own observation of Hero Camp.

137 **The assessors measured the students' knowledge of a variety of concepts:** "Impact of the Heroic Imagination Project Education Programs." Accessed November 29, 2012, from http://heroicimagination.com/resources/reading -room.

138 **"We had to change our approach":** Becca Shipper, in-person interview, May 10, 2011.

139 **It's possibilities like these that have heroism expert Zeno Franco questioning:** Zeno Franco, phone interview, February 7, 2012.

140 **"There's little evidence that knowing about the biases makes you not succumb":** Laurie Santos, in-person interview, July 20, 2011.

CHAPTER NINE: CORPORATE HEROES

143 **Sekerka . . . points to one of her business ethics students:** The firsthand narration in this chapter is based on my observation of Leslie Sekerka's Business Ethics class in which Lynne Henderson presented and led role-plays, Menlo College, Menlo Park, CA, November 1, 2011.

145 **"If you can practice a particular skill":** Lynne Henderson, phone interview, December 6, 2011.

145 **Deterline knows firsthand just how easy it can be:** Brooke Deterline, video presentation during Philip Zimbardo talk, "Inspiring Heroic Leadership in the

NOTES

Boardroom & Senior Management," Stanford University Rock Center for Corporate Governance, May 9, 2012.

147 **when the assistant Mike McQueary saw the Penn State football team's former defensive coordinator:** My summation of the Jerry Sandusky incident is based on a number of media reports, including Peter Durantine, "Penn State's McQueary Tells Court What He Saw," *New York Times*, December 16, 2011. Accessed December 14, 2012, from http://www.nytimes.com/2011/12/17/sports/ncaafootball/mcqueary-testifies-about-sandusky-assault.html.

151 **"I left for a meeting during the session and was immediately able to apply":** Heroic Imagination Project, "Corporate Program Participant Feedback." Accessed November 29, 2012, from http://heroicimagination.org/corporate-overview/testimonials.

151 **People high in what she calls "professional moral courage":** Leslie Sekerka's work on professional moral courage and workplace ethics, which is summarized in this chapter, is described in a variety of sources. They include Leslie Sekerka, Richard Bagozzi, and Richard Charnigo, "Facing Ethical Challenges in the Workplace: Conceptualizing and Measuring Professional Moral Courage," *Journal of Business Ethics* 89, no. 4 (2009): 565–79; Leslie Sekerka, J. Dan McCarthy, and Richard Bagozzi, "Developing the Capacity for Professional Moral Courage: Facing Daily Ethical Challenges in Today's Military Workplace," in D. Comer and G. Vega, eds., *Moral Courage in Organizations: Doing the Right Thing at Work* (Armonk, NY: M. E. Sharpe, 2011), 130–41; and Leslie Sekerka and Lindsey Godwin, "Strengthening Professional Moral Courage: A Balanced Approach to Ethics Training," *Training & Management Development Methods* 24, no. 5 (2010): 63–74. See also Leslie Sekerka, Lindsey Godwin, and Richard Charnigo, "Use of Balanced Experiential Inquiry to Build Ethical Strength in the Workplace," in special issue *Experiential Learning & Management Education* for the *Journal of Management Development* 31, no. 3 (2012): 275–86; and Leslie Sekerka, "Preserving Integrity in the Face of Corruption: Exercising Moral Muscle in the Path to Right Action," *Journal of Organizational Moral Psychology* 1, no. 3 (2011): 1–14.

152 **"You want to be rewarded for doing the right thing":** Leslie Sekerka, phone interview, December 2, 2011.

153 **"This is a developmental model where you learn the skills":** Mary Gentile, phone interview, July 11, 2012.

CHAPTER TEN: REAL-LIFE SUPERHEROES

159 **Chaim Lazaros is getting anxious:** My firsthand narration of events in this chapter, as well as the profiles of various real-life superheroes, are primarily

based on my visit to the Superheroes Anonymous meeting in New York City, October 30, 2011.

162 **"I think all of us wish we could do more about certain situations":** Zeno Franco, phone interview, February 7, 2012.

162 **"On one hand, they probably love being in a position of control":** Jeremy Frimer, phone interview, February 23, 2012.

163 **"I went to the meeting, and I was one of probably thirty people":** Nicole Abramovici ("Prowler"), phone interview, February 20, 2012.

166 **"A costume of any sort is a signal":** Quotes from Robin Rosenberg in this chapter are from my phone interview with her, August 24, 2012.

167 **The 2011 top 10 included Derreck Kayongo:** "And the Top 10 CNN Heroes of 2011 Are . . ." CNN, September 22, 2011. Accessed November 29, 2012, from http://www.cnn.com/2011/LIVING/09/21/cnnheroes.top10/index.html.

CHAPTER ELEVEN: TAKING THE HERO CHALLENGE

173 **By and large, members of the "bravery" group were completely ordinary:** Lawrence J. Walker, Jeremy A. Frimer, et al., "Varieties of Moral Personality: Beyond the Banality of Heroism," *Journal of Personality* 78, no. 3 (2010): 907–42.

174 **"People that do these things are different in subtle ways":** Jeremy Frimer, phone interview, February 23, 2012.

174 **heroes have a tendency to see what happens to them through a redemptive lens:** Lawrence J. Walker and Jeremy A. Frimer, "Moral Personality of Brave and Caring Exemplars," *Journal of Personality and Social Psychology* 93, no. 5 (November 2007): 845–60.

174 **What set the rescuers apart was the way they looked at the world:** Kristen Monroe, "Cracking the Code of Genocide: The Moral Psychology of Rescuers, Bystanders, and Nazis during the Holocaust," *Political Psychology* 29, no. 5 (October 2008): 699–736.

175 **A study of thirty-two "physical heroes":** Ted Huston et al., "Bystander Intervention into Crime: A Study Based on Naturally-Occurring Episodes," *Social Psychology Quarterly* 44, no. 1 (1981): 14–23.

176 **The video highlights something I never realized:** Heroic Imagination Project, "Stanley Milgram: Obedience to Authority" video. Accessed December 19, 2012, from http://heroicimagination.org/research/situational-awareness/social -influence-forces/obedience-to-authority.

177 **Another video recounts the cautionary tale:** Heroic Imagination Project, "Bystander Effect—Death of Matthew Carrington" video. Accessed December 19, 2012, http://www.youtube.com/watch?v=Kt_ZtfhQ094.

185 **"There's a high correlation between volunteering significantly, sixty hours a year":** Philip Zimbardo, Skype interview, September 24, 2012.

186 **Generally, the more hours people spend volunteering:** Office of Research and Policy Development, Corporation for National and Community Service, "The Health Benefits of Volunteering: A Review of Recent Research." Accessed December 19, 2012, from www2.illinois.gov/serve/Documents/Health_Benefits _Volunteering.pdf.

186 **The psychologist Robin Rosenberg points out:** Robin Rosenberg, phone interview, August 24, 2012.

CHAPTER TWELVE: CULTIVATING A HEROIC LIFE

191 **In the year 2002, Christoph von Toggenburg embarked on an audacious journey:** My telling of Christoph von Toggenburg's life story throughout this chapter is based primarily on my Skype interview with him, October 12, 2011.

194 **"Fifty percent is genetic and ten percent environmental":** Dacher Keltner, in-person interview, August 10, 2011, and follow-up e-mail.

195 **"Self-control partly evolved to enable us to do altruistic things":** Roy Baumeister, phone interview, December 5, 2011.

197 **when people feel more secure in their relationships:** Mario Mikulincer and Phillip Shaver, "Attachment Security, Compassion, and Altruism," *Current Directions in Psychological Science* 14, no. 1 (February 2005): 34–38.

197 **When Samuel Oliner, himself a Holocaust survivor:** Samuel Oliner and Pearl Oliner, *The Altruistic Personality: Rescuers of Jews in Nazi Europe* (New York: Free Press, 1988).

198 **"When I think about how people can be altruistic or kind":** Rudy Mendoza-Denton, phone interview, May 10, 2011.

198 **DeSteno and his colleagues told experimental subjects they were doing a study on musical perception:** David DeSteno, presentation, "Science of Compassion" conference presented by the Center for Compassion and Altruism Research and Education. Telluride, CO, July 22–25, 2012.

199 **According to the UCLA School of Medicine psychiatrist Jeffrey Schwartz:** Jeffrey Schwartz, phone interview, November 11, 2011.

201 **"That's how I see the heroic imagination—a visualization process":** Zeno Franco, phone interview, February 7, 2012.

201 **Such a code was preeminent in Old English society:** Clinton Albertson, *Anglo-Saxon Saints and Heroes* (New York: Fordham University Press, 1967).

201 **The presence of a clearly defined company code of ethics:** Janet S. Adams et al., "Codes of Ethics as Signals for Ethical Behavior," *Journal of Business Ethics* 29, no. 3 (February 2001).

202 **moral codes that demanded sacrifice to causes larger than any individual:** David Brooks, "The Organization Kid," *Atlantic Monthly*, April 2001. Accessed December 3, 2012, from http://www.theatlantic.com/magazine/archive/2001 /04/the-organization-kid/302164.

203 **popularized by the lawyer Cass Sunstein and the economist Richard Thaler:** Richard Thaler and Cass Sunstein, *Nudge: Improving Decisions About Health, Wealth, and Happiness* (New Haven: Yale University Press, 2008).

203 **"Given that we have certain social goals":** Laurie Santos, in-person interview, July 20, 2011.

203 **Another example is the Yahoo-powered accessory search engine good search.com:** "About Us/FAQ," Goodsearch. Accessed December 17, 2012, from http://www.goodsearch.com/about.aspx#faq1.

205 **Robin Williams's character, the English teacher John Keating:** *Dead Poets Society*. Film. Dir. Peter Weir. Touchstone Pictures, 1989.